THE WAY OF THE
hammock

Hay House Titles of Related Interest

YOU CAN HEAL YOUR LIFE, the movie, starring Louise Hay & Friends
(available as a 1-DVD program and an expanded 2-DVD set)
Watch the trailer at: www.LouiseHayMovie.com

THE SHIFT, the movie, starring Dr. Wayne W. Dyer
(available as a 1-DVD program and an expanded 2-DVD set)
Watch the trailer at: www.DyerMovie.com

❧

*AWAKENING THE LUMINOUS MIND: Tibetan Meditation
for Inner Peace and Joy,* by Tenzin Wangyal Rinpoche

*BECOMING AWARE: How to Repattern Your Brain and Revitalize
Your Life,* by Lisa Garr

LIFE LOVES YOU: 7 Spiritual Practices to Heal Your Life,
by Louise Hay and Robert Holden

*MEET YOUR SOUL: A Powerful Guide to Connect with Your Most
Sacred Self,* by Elisa Romeo

*THE MOTIVATION MANIFESTO: 9 Declarations to Claim Your
Personal Power,* by Brendon Burchard

All of the above are available at your local bookstore,
or may be ordered by visiting:

Hay House USA: www.hayhouse.com®
Hay House Australia: www.hayhouse.com.au
Hay House UK: www.hayhouse.co.uk
Hay House South Africa: www.hayhouse.co.za
Hay House India: www.hayhouse.co.in

THE WAY OF THE
hammock
DESIGNING CALM FOR A BUSY LIFE

Marga Odahowski

HAY HOUSE, INC.
Carlsbad, California • New York City
London • Sydney • Johannesburg
Vancouver • Hong Kong • New Delhi

Copyright © 2015 by Marga Odahowski

Published and distributed in the United States by: Hay House, Inc.: www.hayhouse.com® • **Published and distributed in Australia by:** Hay House Australia Pty. Ltd.: www.hayhouse.com.au • **Published and distributed in the United Kingdom by:** Hay House UK, Ltd.: www .hayhouse.co.uk • **Published and distributed in the Republic of South Africa by:** Hay House SA (Pty), Ltd.: info@hayhouse.co.za • **Distributed in Canada by:** Raincoast Books: www.raincoast.com • **Published in India by:** Hay House Publishers India: www .hayhouse.co.in

Cover design: Angela Moody and Mary Michaela Murray
Interior design: Nick C. Welch

Library of Congress Cataloging-in-Publication Data
Odahowski, Marga, date.
The way of the hammock : designing calm for a busy life / Marga Odahowski.
    pages cm
  ISBN 978-1-4019-4407-0 (paperback)
1. Calmness. 2. Relaxation. I. Title.
BF575.C35O33 2015
158.1--dc23

                                        2015001050

Tradepaper ISBN: 978-1-4019-4407-0

10 9 8 7 6 5 4 3 2 1

1st edition, June 2015

Printed in the United States of America

SUSTAINABLE FORESTRY INITIATIVE
Certified Chain of Custody
Promoting Sustainable Forestry
www.sfiprogram.org
SFI-01268

SFI label applies to text stock

For my parents,
William and Mary Jo Odahowski

contents

preface

A sign caught my eye in an Italian airport a few years ago:

"ARRIVING DAILY, INNER PEACE."

I embraced this message with a smile. My career has been dedicated to understanding the mind-body connection as a path to inner peace, and I'm continually discovering research that embraces the idea that peace is available to all of us. With the right tools and practices, we can claim a peaceful state of mind.

Everyone I know—students, professors, friends, parents, farmers, executives, and others—is busy, stressed, and overscheduled. My friends in the business world live a frantic life filled with deadlines and endless meetings, e-mails, and texting. The societal pressure to achieve through *doing* more is pervasive in our world. Even my Italian friends are finding it harder to claim *la dolce vita*, the sweet life.

With today's distractions, we must seek the inner technologies of relaxation, mindfulness, and positivity to keep us focused and on track. While these practices of calm may be new to many of you, I studied, practiced, and taught mindfulness in both my work and in my personal life for the past 30 years. I earned a master's degree in counseling; and I have worked as a counselor, health educator, university professor, and mindfulness consultant. Teaching these skills that transform lives has been one of my deepest joys in my career.

One of my greatest learning experiences as a counselor was working in an alcohol and drug rehabilitation hospital in Spofford, New Hampshire. I realized that what people needed most of all was a set of integrated skills to navigate life's demands. I switched careers to health promotion so I could impact more individuals by teaching skills that not only created a healthy lifestyle, but also a *mind style* of creativity.

Later, as the Director of Studies for the International Residential College at the University of Virginia, I began teaching academic courses on *mindful leadership*. I married my love of design with mindfulness, which resulted in a process that not only generated calm, but also enhanced creativity. The three areas of well-researched practices I used were relaxation, mindfulness, and positivity. Along with design skills, they supported my students in sustaining behavior changes that enhance wellness, leadership, and creativity. Being creative requires awareness, empathy, collaboration, and decision making; and these same qualities are needed in leadership and life. The calm mind-set creates the openness to be flexible to new thinking, ideas, and possibilities.

Today I teach modern mindfulness programs for corporations and organizations around the world. I continue to use design thinking, the inner technologies of soothing relaxation and mindful awareness, and directing the mind to positive action in the development of compassionate and effective leaders.

~

I wasn't always like this. Like many of you, I was stressed out and looking for solutions to live a more balanced life. My mind-set many years ago was that there was something wrong with me and I needed to fix it. Now I'd like to share with you my early journey to discovering these skills of calm.

It was over 30 years ago when I attended a career workshop in Stevens Point, Wisconsin, at the National Wellness Institute. The instructor introduced me to many inner strategies to help me become more focused in my life and career. At the age of 25, I felt the need to reflect, *I've lived a quarter century. What am I going to do with this life?* The instructor asked us to write down the names of three people who would guide us on our life's journey. I wrote Goldie Hawn, the Dalai Lama, and Albert Einstein. Next she asked us to write about the qualities they each embodied.

I wrote:

Goldie Hawn for joy.
The Dalai Lama for compassion.
Albert Einstein for brilliance.

She stated: "The three qualities you picked are already within you. You only need to discover and develop them."

During the workshop, the instructor introduced me to many practices, including relaxation, mindfulness, and positivity. These practices had such a significant impact on me that I wrote a short essay on what I had accomplished and experienced during the past 25 years and what I was going to do with my life in the future. Over the years, the three elements of joy, compassion, and brilliance became the essential heart and core of my teaching and my life's path.

The career workshop I took over 25 years ago became a faded memory until one cold winter afternoon when I opened my computer at my university office and found an e-mail from Goldie Hawn. I was surprised!

Goldie wrote a beautiful note of support, complimenting me on my Mindful Leadership course at the University of Virginia. Goldie had participated in the Mind and Life Dialogues on Compassion program with one of the University of Virginia's esteemed Religious Studies faculty, Jeffrey Hopkins. She had heard about my work from my colleague, Jeffrey Walker, who consulted with Hopkins on the Mindful Leadership course we were co-developing for the University of Virginia's McIntire School of Commerce.

Goldie was on a similar path, introducing practices of calm into early childhood education. She was developing the Hawn Foundation, an organization focusing on improving children's abilities to learn and thrive by teaching them social and emotional literacy skills that improve academic performance and give children and teachers a set of tools to lead smart, healthy, happier lives.

During our initial interactions, I quickly recognized that Goldie's brilliance extended beyond her amazing ability to entertain. Goldie's work championing social and emotional learning for elementary education through the Hawn Foundation was helping shape the future of education. Goldie and I shared research findings and stories about our endeavors toward developing curricula for children and young adults to cultivate empathy, compassion, and self-efficacy (the belief of one's ability to succeed).

Eventually, in 2004, she invited me to attend the Educating from the Heart conference that was held in Vancouver, British Columbia. The keynote presenter was His Holiness the Dalai Lama. I was thrilled to attend. This would be the first time I'd see Goldie and the Dalai Lama in person. Her kindness and generous heart shone as we spent time at the event and at her home.

During the event I met the publisher of a mind-body-spirit magazine called *Common Boundary*. I had not heard of the magazine, but less than 20 minutes later, I went to the ladies' room and found a copy someone had left there. On the cover of the magazine was a picture of Albert Einstein, and in this synchronistic moment, I remembered the workshop 30 years earlier when I wrote down the names of the three people who would guide my life. This led me to reflect on the commonalities of the work of Albert Einstein, the Dalai Lama, and Goldie Hawn. They all have a sense of joy, commitment to compassion, and brilliance in their fearless efforts toward sharing transformational information.

This serendipitous meeting anchored my resolve to share transforming skills with people. I returned to my work as a university faculty member with a renewed vigor to support my students by teaching modern life skills to slow down, change their relationship to stress, create life-serving habits, and connect with their innate well-being.

I embraced this positive approach to personal and professional development in my curriculum. I shared practices with my students that support well-being, and I encouraged them to design their own lifestyle habits of calm and share them with others. I used these evidence-based practices to make the classroom come alive and to see if my students would shift from surviving to thriving.

I often ask my students at the beginning of the semester, "If you could learn one thing from this class, what would it be?"

My students almost always answer, "How can I relax and make good choices?"

They are so stressed out they *can't make decisions.*

It was my students who encouraged me to write this book. After taking my class, they would often say something like: "I gained skills for a lifetime. This is the best class I have taken at the university." Even years later, many contact me to share their gratitude for learning skills that continue to assist them in their day-to-day lives.

The Way of the Hammock provides a busy person with an enjoyable and practical way to build the skills of joy, compassion, and brilliance. In this book, I offer a process to emphasize the value of forming a designer's mind-set to enhance your lifestyle and bring ease to decision making and creativity.

I wrote this book as an everyday tool for transformation, and I hope it becomes a personal and practical resource for you. If you have struggled with change, then this book is for you. It draws from health science, design, and, most important, your inner wisdom to create sustainable change. My hope for you is that this book inspires you and aids you in creating a life of joy, compassion, and brilliance.

introduction

As a kid, the hammock was my haven, a place I could go to be by myself but also to be myself. I recall those summer days in Wisconsin tucked in the hammock at our summer house on Lake Geneva. I savored my daily idyll, breathing in the sweetness of fresh-cut grass in the air. This time alone brought me back to myself. I let the world go. I let my imagination soar. I received insights and inspiration.

Later, when I taught at the University of Virginia, I'd walk around the historic grounds and see students relaxing in hammocks, enjoying the summer warmth. Once, when walking by a group taking a tour, I overheard a mother say to her son, "Honey, if you are going to fit in here, you are going to have to wear flip-flops." As I strolled further down the colonnade, I saw a pack of students all sporting flip-flops; the mother was right. I have to admit, just seeing those shoes on my students caused a relaxed feeling to come over me. I wanted a pair. I went to my friend's local shoe shop, Scarpa, and the perfect pair of silver Mephistos won me over. I loved the relaxed feel and the ease of slipping them on and off. When I wore these humble shoes, I noticed they literally slowed me down.

I believe we all look for ways to slow down. Today, however, we need more than flip-flops. We need tangible ways to let go of the strain caused by the many demands throughout the day. Just like conforming to the relatively recent fashion of flip-flops, many of us conform to the culture of stress, feeling the need to act quickly as a reaction to the pace of our hectic world.

There is so much pressure to do more, and a pervasive feeling of not having enough time. All of this results in taking on too much and then resorting to ineffective multitasking. We find ourselves spinning in cycles of stress and despair. I hear my students express this all the time.

When I ask, "How are you?" they reply, "Busy—I can't wait for school to end so I can relax."

But school leads to work and a career. "Busy" never ends.

We've all received e-mail offers and seen ads that say things like: "Act now for this limited-time offer," "You'd better be quick!" and "Hurry—time is running out." These messages echo throughout our society. Marketing experts know that creating tension in decision making motivates people to buy. This type of promotion creates anxiety or a sense of urgency, playing with our feelings—our fear of missing out and our "I'm so busy" mind-set. When I allow myself to get caught up in these marketing messages, it simply creates more for my to-do list.

This rush to decide leads to decision fatigue. It is the sluggish feeling that hits when too many choices are presented and the mind freezes. It becomes impossible to decide. That feeling of indecisiveness can be exhausting. This is what my university students experience, and they want solutions to help them make quick, clear decisions.

Have you ever suffered from decision fatigue? I think we all have experienced this at some point in our lives, especially when we are overcommitted. We only have so much mental energy in one day. How we design our day can make a world of difference. When we have hectic schedules and are not rested, hydrated, or nourished, our willpower and our ability to make wise decisions diminish.

It is that feeling you get when you look at the cereal aisle in the grocery store. You have made decisions all day and now the cereal aisle provides too many choices. You stand there frozen with indecision. When you're tired, overcommitted, and overwhelmed with so much to do, even deciding what cereal to buy seems like an impossible choice.

This state was my norm during my college years, as an undergraduate at the University of Wisconsin in Stevens Point, home of the National Wellness Institute. I lacked willpower. Decisions were difficult. Yet the wellness movement intrigued me; I thought it'd be the cure to the stress I was experiencing as a student. My interest in the integrated-wellness lifestyle increased as I listened to gurus in the field of mind-body medicine. I majored in sociology with an emphasis on art and social work. In my classes, I learned that willpower is physiological and limited—what I needed was *skillpower.*

I craved a life that was relaxed, productive, and energized, and also included time for family and friends. I experimented with practices and looked to the great leaders to help me learn new skills. I learned about the Mind and Life Institute where the Dalai Lama collaborates with the top researchers of the world in the science of relaxation, compassion, and happiness. The year I attended the Mind and Life Institute, His Holiness met with Dr. Richard Davidson from the University of Wisconsin, Jon Kabat-Zinn from the University of Massachusetts, and others to discuss how the practice of cultivating positive emotions has an impact on our well-being.

I took my first yoga class while in graduate school for a master's degree in counseling. The class was taught after work in the Mental Health Center where I had my internship. In this small-group practice of yoga, I learned the value of stillness and quiet in my daily routine. This led to my teaching relaxation to faculty at the University of Wisconsin in 1983.

At the time, it surprised me that so many people needed the skills to achieve calm. Today, we have access to substantial evidence-based research confirming that the way to a smart mind is a quiet mind. The neuroscience of meditation shows that it reduces cortisol, a stress hormone with many negative effects on the body.

His Holiness, who describes himself as a simple monk, often speaks about the two ways to create happiness. The first way is external, through finding better— better clothes, better flip-flops, better friends, better jobs . . . changing the outside situation of our lives. External happiness is not bad, but it doesn't last long. It's like a pedicure that makes happy feet for a few days but fades with time. For true, sustainable change, we need mind-set skills, new habits, and support—a tribe of friends.

Years ago, one of my external fixes was daydreaming of moving to Montana; I was certain that life was more relaxed in the West. I even applied to and got offered a job in Bozeman, Montana. But then I realized that my life and work there would be the same as it always had been. I was still in a reactive state; looking for external sources to help with my daily stressors. What I learned in the process of applying for this job out West was that I could create new opportunities for my work and life even while staying right where I was. The interview process shifted my mind-set. I became an *intra*preneur—I leveraged my current position within the University of Virginia to create change within my workplace *and* myself.

This leads me to the second way to happiness: accepting the responsibility to understand our inner development, which then creates sustainable joy, what I think of as abiding grace. I tiptoed around this inner source of happiness for several years, thinking I would have to do things like travel to India, meet a guru, and learn a mantra. I liked yoga, but I wasn't ready to give up my Western ways.

Then, one day, I remembered the hammock.

The memories of my summer days of happiness called back to me the desire for calm. The sounds of the rustling leaves and the touch of the light breeze on my skin brought me back to my senses. I needed to get a hammock to re-create this soothing quality. When I watched the clouds drift by, time slowed down.

I didn't need to go West and escape to a ranch; the hammock would be my modern refuge. I found myself daydreaming about this for months. I imagined how it looked and how I would feel lying in it. I remembered the warmth of the sun touching my skin and the fragrance of nearby evergreens, which made me smile with happiness. It brought back memories of being a kid, with all the time in the world. I didn't think of how to go about getting a hammock. As the months passed, I simply saw myself in one, completely relaxed.

Then one day, I noticed a woman in front of me while at my favorite store, T.J.Maxx. It was Gigi, a former colleague, whom I hadn't seen in ten years. As we waited in the checkout line, we got caught up on each other's lives. Just as we were parting, Gigi mentioned she was headed across the street to Lowe's.

I asked, "Do you think they have hammocks?" I described to her how much I loved and wanted one.

She looked at me and said, "I have a great hammock tucked in our shed. We got it as a wedding gift. It's brand new and has never been used. You can have it."

I could not believe it. I was so excited to pick it up and was astounded to find that it was of those deluxe hammocks, double-sized with extra-thick quilted fabric. It even spoke to my aesthetic sensibilities, a solid green on one side and striped on the other. The stand was sturdy and reliable. It was the perfect hammock for my yard! I live in a historic house nestled in the university's famous arboretum, a garden filled with Kentucky coffee trees and Osage orange trees. Not just any hammock could stand next to such greatness, but this one matched the majesty of the extensive gardens.

In my new hammock, I began my daily practice of *undoing.* Time alone was the key. I loved being outside relaxing in nature. My mind and body were soothed as I felt the warm sun and breeze on my skin and heard the sounds of robins and squirrels in the distance. I enjoyed the way my body relaxed. It felt like being held in loving arms. In the hammock, a wave of calmness dissolved my life problems into solutions. The insights seemed to bubble up as I continued to let go and relax. I wasn't thinking about the problems. The solutions arrived unannounced. We all have had these *singing arrivals* miraculously appear to us.

Being in the hammock, lying still, and breathing in silence became my calm practice of just being. From my mental worries to my physical aches and sore muscles, the unraveling continued with each period of time I spent there alone. I had been pushing myself too hard, keeping up with work, family, and the latest fitness crazes. The hammock allowed me to let go. My mental, emotional, and physical body slowly recognized a way back to health. I flourished. The greatest path to contentment and joy is to relax in the love of your being.

Hammock yoga. Do nothing. No guru needed. The only thing required is a commitment to a consistent practice—diligence. I have diligence. I use this quality of determination to achieve many things in my life. Why not use the diligence to create calm?

This regular time in the hammock allowed for undoing. When it was cold outside or my time was limited, my chair, bed, yoga mat, or couch became my alternate indoor hammock.

All I really needed was a dose of quiet time in stillness. My hammock time became my personal practice for relaxation, mindfulness, and positivity.

How to Use This Book

In my training as a health educator, I learned that the best way to make something a habit is to experiment with what works for you. I will teach you how to create rituals and routines to support your practice until it becomes ingrained. For me, it is my hammock practice. For you, it may be something totally different.

This book will cover the foundational living assignments, the *how-to* practices of creating calm throughout your day, and share the value of having a *designer's mind* through keeping a design notebook to provide a daily ritual that supports well-being. Let your practice be your teacher.

Here is an overview of what to expect from each chapter.

1. Think Like a Designer

The beauty and simplicity of this book is that you are the designer of your practice. You can create the habits that are best for you. In Chapter 1, you are introduced to ways to *discover, make,* and *do* things differently, with the playful curiosity of a designer.

I like teaching design practices because they create happiness in the change process. Designers like to play, make mistakes, and see more possibilities in the process. In this book you will learn about three elements of design—discover, make, do—and how to use them in your daily life for effective change and decision making.

Design methods support problem solving by exploring possibilities and taking action. A valuable design tool is to keep a notebook of your ideas, successes, and progress. Writing and drawing help with making your imagination come alive in your day-to-day world. Making images is a way to visualize new ideas and explore positive outcomes.

Today, design thinking is an integral component of problem solving within the fields of education, medicine, and business to support the creation of the best solutions for our health, work, relationships, and community.

2. Relaxation

Active relaxation is a powerful daily practice that allows our body's natural intelligence to work. Calming the mind and body is the foundation of all the other methods in the book. When I take time for moments of relaxation throughout the day, it profoundly impacts my decision making, effectiveness, and productivity. Building supportive relaxation habits, which include drinking water, eating real food, and getting a good night's sleep, assists our body in fully and deeply relaxing.

You can begin anywhere when it comes to adding in more relaxation to your daily routine. Try using the design elements of discover, make, and do to explore practices that invite calm moments into your daily routine.

Relaxation provides energy and allows the grace of sustainable joy. Chapter 2 teaches the foundational lifestyle habits of breathing and stretching that shift us from thinking to being. Relaxation gets us out of our head and into our body.

3. Mindfulness

Mindfulness reconnects us with our habits and routines. As we do things in our day-to-day environment, our actions become automatic, unconscious reactions. Mindfulness awakens us, causing us to become aware once again of our habits. This helps us change our relationship to them. Mindfulness is a relationship builder. You develop a relationship with your mind and body and in doing so you learn to discern and act effectively.

Self-kindness, compassion, and curiosity are all qualities of mindfulness that transform unconscious habits effectively. Paying attention with kindness to ourselves creates a new level of self-care that is restorative and builds resiliency. Self-kindness helps change our relationship to stress through allowing us to accept our feelings and let them go with compassion.

Chapter 3 shows the value in your daily life of cultivating the qualities of awareness, acceptance, and compassion. When practicing mindfulness, we realize that these qualities are the core of all creativity. You'll be able to use the design processes of discover, make, and do as mindfulness practices to heighten your ability to self-regulate emotions and step out of fear.

4. Positivity

Positive psychology focuses on cultivating emotions that create well-being and meaning in our lives. A focus on the positive directs our mind and actions toward meaning and connection and supports us in our daily lives by connecting us to calmness and creativity. You'll use the design practices of discover, make, and do to build positive emotions that make a significant impact on enjoying and savoring your day.

Chapter 4 explains the value that optimistic, encouraging, and constructive emotions have on tapping into your intuition, the voice of inner wisdom. The wise self says, "Relax, stay home, and read a book." Positivity is the key to keeping calm, a state of mind that results in greater clarity for decision making.

5. Nudges

The best way to begin a new practice is to create daily rituals and routines that fit nicely into your current lifestyle. Chapter 5 includes a sample of assignments I have given my students and clients over 15 years of teaching. For the purpose of this book, I have called them "nudges." Each nudge is a simple, natural practice that easily fits into your day.

Are you thinking, *I'm too busy for this*? Know that taking action can be as simple as practicing for five minutes a day. Small practices build discipline.

My students and I start with a one-minute practice. We begin with a way of *being* rather than thinking or doing. My class starts with a one-minute breathing awareness practice, a "noticing the breath in the body" exercise. We continue to do this at the beginning of every class, and I ask them to do this on their own throughout the week.

To create a new daily ritual for them, I suggest they add a longer breathing exercise to an already-established habit in their current routine. For example, I might suggest doing it as they get ready in the morning. Or perhaps they do it walking to and from class or a meeting; when they arrive, they are refreshed and focused. This ten-minute time of breathing awareness can get you out of your head and into your body, allowing for a shift in energy that is restorative.

In Chapter 5, you will learn why the best practices are small, daily, and happy. When we do something we enjoy every day, even for one minute, we build the momentum for change. Let's keep it simple, easy, and doable.

Making the Most of This Book

You may have heard the helpful mantra, "Actions bring results." I designed this book as a tool for action to create tangible results. A big part of how this works includes spending time discovering, making, and doing the practices in this book to build the skills of relaxation, mindfulness, and positivity. This book provides a guide to *undoing.* Take some time to read the entire book through, then experiment with the practices and activities.

Begin a Design Notebook

Keep a daily notebook to explore the practices in this book and as a helpful part of your routine. Frequency builds habit. Designers take note of their ideas, actions, trials and errors, and successes. This creates the mind-set of "continual progress" rather than a striving for "perfection." A notebook gives you a place to doodle, list, plan out, and reflect on how you integrated meaning and well-being into your day, as well as the insights that arrive when you connect with silence.

I keep a Moleskine notebook and Sharpie pen in my bag at all times. Inspiration can arrive anytime and the more I write, the more insightful thoughts emerge. Some of the things I write about include what is working, dream interpretations, insights, to-do lists, and new business ideas. Sometimes I doodle. The ritual of writing is a designer's gold mine.

Pick a Practice

I teach these practices to a variety of audiences: first-year college students, MBA executives, clients I coach, stay-at-home parents, and entrepreneurs. I see the effect they have on so many lives. Positive results happen with regular commitment to reflection before taking inspired and meaningful action.

The value of combining design tools with calming practices is that this creates a simple, doable method for establishing a personal style of calm in your daily life. These practices are for everyone. They build *skillpower* for transformational change.

Receive the Benefits

Here are some of the benefits of applying the strategies contained in *The Way of the Hammock:*

- Increased mental focus, concentration, and decision making

- Increased self-awareness through ongoing self-reflection

- Improved resilience by developing healthy responses to stressful situations

- Enhanced energy and vitality through nutrition, exercise, and adequate sleep

- Improved resourcefulness and creativity

Instead of conforming to a culture of stress, looking for external sources for happiness, this book helps you to design and experience an effective way to relate to everyday distractions and pressures. Your inner brilliance is a valuable guide, and this book gives you the tools to get to that calm mind so you have the confidence and clarity to make effective day-to-day decisions.

Many of these benefits will have a direct impact on your performance at work, school, or home. You might find improvements in your relationships with others as you become more compassionate and grateful. Take responsibility for making healthy lifestyle habits part of your day and building your confidence. As you take small daily steps in creating healthy habits, you will experience more energy, enthusiasm, and vitality.

Use the activities in the book as a guide to incorporating some calm habits into your current life. See what a difference they make in your life and work.

∾∾

think like a designer

DISCOVER, MAKE, DO

In this chapter, I will help you use tools to create a "design mind-set" as you move through the process of creating calm in your life. We achieve our best results in life and work when we are relaxed. The creative mind gets inspiration from stillness, beauty, and connection.

All designers are doers, but good designers understand the value of *not* doing. They take time for discovery by observation, searching for connections and meaning and recognizing opportunities. Think of yourself as a designer; be intentional about structuring your day with practices that support your well-being.

Early in my career I was overwhelmed and thought I did not "have time" to take care of myself. Indeed, it may seem counterintuitive in our busy world that taking time to relax will help us to be productive. The truth is that when we practice active relaxation—with or without a hammock—we are changing our brain's neural pathways, creating a calmer mind. Our perception widens, allowing us to consider the best possibilities. It is essential not only for designers but for all of us to cultivate the qualities that build flexibility and foster a lighthearted nature.

While there are many elements of the design process, the ones I have chosen to focus on are *design discovery, design making*, and *design doing*. I like these three for creating a lifestyle of calm. The design process puts your goals into action. It is a structured approach to generating and evolving ideas for change, decision making, and creating a lifestyle of calm. The design process relies on the ability to be observant, intuitive, and develop new ideas that are meaningful.

Start a Design Notebook

The elements of design have given me tools and empowerment to create meaningful change in my life. One of the habits of a designer is to create daily rituals of creative expression.

Keeping a notebook of your ideas, successes, and progress is a valuable design tool. Writing helps make your imagination come alive in your day-to-day world. Start with making a list, drawing, or collecting a group of magazine pictures of your positive motivations. Use your notebook to write about the results your relaxation practice has on enhancing inspiration and insights.

Writing, drawing, and doodling in a notebook is a practice I have been doing since high school. It has supported both my academic and personal development. When you write, you are honing your skills as a rational thinker as you review your personal choices and decision making.

A design notebook anchors your ideas and provides a place for your inner self to speak freely. Time alone introduces us to our wisdom. You will find the answers to where and how to begin this quest for calm. This is also a place to document your insights and intuitive hits. There are many ways to keep a notebook. I like to use mine for reflection, intention, gratitude, and sharpening my intuition.

An easy way to begin is to simply write one word. I'll often write one word I want to focus on for the day, such as *appreciation*. Then as the day goes on, I continually bring it to mind. This increases my thoughts of appreciation and directs my actions throughout the day.

If you are new to keeping a notebook, you can start with a daily gratitude word. Who and what do you appreciate and how? Write out the details.

Oprah Winfrey turned quite a few of us on to the power of gratitude years ago. I remember when she got so many of us journaling about it. It was awesome. Even though I'd been writing in a journal for years, all my writings had been about "poor me, wah, wah, wah." When I switched to writing about gratitude, my world transformed. I'm not saying you should never grumble. Just do it once and move on to taking the next, best steps to turn a grumble into gratitude.

Personal development and entrepreneurship guru Marie Forleo recently reminded me, "The dividends are in the details." On her show, *MarieTV,* she recently shared the research of Robert Emmons, a psychologist who does gratitude research. Emmons's research suggests that writing detailed accounts of gratitude provides greater value. The more specific you are in your writing, the more powerful it is in creating a sustainable feeling of gratefulness. Marie also shared why writing in a notebook is amazingly helpful. First of all it is a practice that hones discipline. Secondly, keeping a notebook is a great way to unravel personal insights and unwire negative patterns of thinking. By writing daily in your notebook, you have a place to reflect, process, record, and create.

The First Element of Design: Design Discovery

The design tool of discovery helps us get focused and motivated for the changes we want to make. The design discovery process includes:

- Creating a space for alone time
- Asking questions
- Reflecting and gathering inspiration and insights

Discovery is uncovering what wants to be known. It comes from being curious, reflective, and receptive. Understanding the challenges you face is the first step toward discovering what works best for you in creating the lifestyle of calm you desire. Taking time for reflection, we get new insights. Our best inspiration happens when we are both motivated and quiet. Discovery requires that we take time to relax, reflect, explore, and create a meaningful intention. Our intentions are drawn through observation and insights and provide us with the motivation, focus, or direction we need to sustain the change process. Designers are trained in the practice of reflection in order to discover something.

Jeffrey Hopkins, a professor of religious studies at the University of Virginia, has visited my class several times to discuss the power of quieting the mind through a breathing-awareness practice. (Hopkins, who wrote the book *Cultivating Compassion,* was an interpreter for His Holiness the Dalai Lama for ten years. He now does translations for His Holiness.) He told my students to find a meditation they like and practice for just one minute. Make it an easy, pleasurable experience to design new habits and incorporate them into your life. "Stop while you still enjoy it and then gradually increase the time to two minutes and so on," Hopkins says. Wise advice.

Hopkins has also shared with my class the importance of discovering your motivation. To reflect on your personal motivations for getting calm, ask yourself the following questions and write about it in your design notebook:

- *Why is creating compassion and calm a meaningful endeavor for me?*

- *What do I hope to gain by becoming more centered, relaxed, and positive?*

- *How would my calmness affect those around me?*

Imagine how your relationships might change if you were able to relax and center yourself and live with intent. In my Mindful Leadership course at the University of Virginia McIntire School of Commerce, I had a student who felt a true motivation to create a meaningful compassion practice. Kristin shared, "I'm short-tempered, and I thought I inherited it from my mother. I now realize I have a choice. I don't have to be short-tempered. When I feel anger arise, I use my breathing to calm me. This new mindfulness approach allows me to accept my anger and respond more effectively."

Discovery is the first part of the change process. All Kristin needed to change was her relationship to her feelings of frustration. As we worked together over the semester, she gained the awareness and insight to befriend her emotions with some self-compassion, thus eliminating angry outbursts, yet honoring her feelings and seeing their source. Kristin ended the semester amazed and relieved. Two things shifted for her; one was her belief about herself and the other was her relationship with her feelings. She was now able to befriend her emotions—and with that, they dissolved. Can you imagine how changing a habit of being short-tempered would change her relationships at home and work? What might you discover if you slow down and begin to pay attention?

Kristin had a strong intention for changing her relationship with her anger. Learning to allow room for reflection and discovery creates motivation, allowing insights to emerge. Trusting your inner wisdom will strengthen it over time as you use it. When I practice calm and compassion, I am not only benefiting myself by making better decisions, but I am also helping my family, friends, neighbors, and the community. As I extend kindness to myself, I have found it easier to extend this to others.

After you have taken some time in discovery, you can move to design making where you tap into your imagination to make your ideas expand and come alive with visualization, images, and models.

Find Your Motivation

Take a moment to reflect on your personal motivation for increased well-being. More peace of mind, compassion, self-kindness, and discernment are some possible motivations. Imagine and feel the value and meaning that flourishing will have on your life. Having a genuine intention, motivation, and purpose will assist you in discovering your practice. If habits are part of our human nature, why not cultivate habits that enhance our life and well-being?

We all get preoccupied sometimes. We fail to slow down and be in the moment. How often have you been in a conversation with someone without being fully present? Our mind is thinking about other things that need to get done: a dinner that needs to be cooked, a project that still needs attention, or work e-mails we need to catch up on. Ironically, this often leads to more work later, as we are not fully present in our communications. When we are present, we can get things done efficiently in a calm and productive manner. And when we are actually present, we can make more effective decisions. A calm practice is a daily system of developing this ability of presence and discovery.

Knowing your motivations for increased well-being allows you to create clear and consistent intentions. A clear intention allows you to discover what the *doable* is at the moment. The doable is the unique right action for you to create your desired outcome. There is no cookie-cutter approach. This is the beauty of design and discovery.

As you use these processes over time, you tap into your intuitive knowledge, which is the quickest and most direct path toward your outcome. Stop looking for answers and ask more questions. Use the power of intention and reflection to guide your discovery.

As things become more complex, asking questions can lead to real insight and inspiration. Genuine questions release your creativity and vulnerability, attracting more perspectives and possibilities. I love asking myself a question and then just sitting in my hammock, daydreaming and relaxing. For instance, I might ask myself, *Which project needs my attention? Who do I need to connect with this week? What foods do I need to add or eliminate from my diet?*

Then, like clouds in the sky floating by, the answer arrives. This time of letting go allows the brain to function effectively. While you are relaxing, it is making connections and doing the work to let some insights bubble up.

You can easily create a daily practice of creating and sustaining calm, but you have to make it unique to you. Make it your own. The details don't matter as much; consistency is what works.

The Second Element of Design: Design Making

Once you have uncovered your motivation and have clear intentions for a calm lifestyle, you can move to making. In this second element of the design process, we focus on making by using your imagination and creating prototypes.

Use Your Imagination

You can start with daydreaming as a simple form of making. This allows your imagination to explore your ideas using different points of view.

Then, create a tangible representation of your imagination, even in the smallest of ways, by making a model. You can begin simply by writing in a notebook. Your calm, creative mind will let you see possibilities and at the same time help you make a clear decision.

One imagination-building activity I use in my note-book is to daydream and write about my perfect day. I just fill the page with how I would like my calm and productive time to look. I use writing to imagine my house and my office, how I interact with my family and friends, and what activities fill my hours.

For example, in writing this book I imagined my perfect writing day that included brain breaks full of nature, beauty, and the opportunity to connect with others. It took me a while to find the perfect writing spot outside of my home office. One day I came across a café that has been the perfect match for this book project and fulfills those needs I wrote about.

As I write this, I'm sitting at Shark Mountain Coffee located at the Innovation Lab at the University of Virginia Darden School of Business. It is a quiet coffee shop with a great modern vibe. The music is subtle and gentle for minds that are writing. I surround myself with the other patrons, entrepreneurs, hipster students, faculty, and yogis who are all working on creative projects. Johnny, the owner, is making chocolate bars in between coffee orders. I am a fan of his music and pu-erh tea.

This place is my office away from home, a great place to write and connect. I am productive in my writing and take breaks outside in nature or with new people who connect me to the next great opportunity to share my work.

I schedule time to write or edit at Shark Mountain Coffee because it is the place I am most productive and happy.

Writing a book has made me reflect on my energy levels and experiment with the best times of the day to do my writing. The process of making includes accidents and mistakes. No need for perfection—just be present. Make progress.

When I began to experiment with different times of the day and different places to write, I realized the morning and midday were my best times. This helped me plan my schedule, and I blocked out these times in my calendar. I made a wall calendar to show me the weeks and month. I balance other projects in the late afternoon and evening. Making the wall calendar helped me visualize my deadline as I crossed off the passing days.

Use Images

Imagination and visualization are powerful tools in design making. By creating images in your mind and connecting emotionally with them, you begin to direct your attention to the positive. This gives you the fuel to take inspired action when the time is right. In imaging, you have a chance to refine your ideas over time.

If image-creation in your mind is difficult for you, try using photographs or cutting pictures from magazines. Pick images that have meaning and bring a feeling of power, connection, and possibilities. You can use modern technology to archive your images; websites and apps such as Facebook, Instagram, and Pinterest can support your creativity. Spend your time with the people who share your values. Another great place to have relaxing images is on your screen saver. All of these are subtle yet powerful reminders of the relaxation state we want to encourage.

The mind loves images. Visualize health or lifestyle outcomes for yourself, along with the steps to get there. You enhance the effectiveness of the change process when you step into the picture of your life. Notice the colors, sensations, and smells, the feeling of warm sunlight on your skin, a bright blue sky, and a hot bath. Imagining is not only seeing but also feeling the result. Imagination takes practice. Try starting at the end. Imagination is a way to hone your focus.

What outcome do you want to create? What do you imagine it to be? Mentally craft your ideal life situation. Use all your senses. What would it look like, feel like, and sound like? Form a picture in your mind and a feeling in your body.

Take some time to write and describe in detail your ideas in your notebook. Do this in extreme detail and repeat every few months. This is part of the making. Next, begin to shift your inner dialogue to support this new version of yourself and your life. Create a collage, folder, or vision board. (I'll describe how to do so in Chapter 5.) The activities in this book will not only help you imagine your best self, they will help you build qualities that support well-being by giving you the tools and skills you need.

For example, for many years I kept a folder and made collages about where I wanted to live and what opportunities I wanted to experience. Every time I saw an article about a city or career that interested me, I would clip it and put it in my folder. I would daydream about moving to the city or having that job. Occasionally, I looked at my folder and savored the images and words. Many years later, I found my way to that city! (Later in the book, I share the story of how I got there by listening to my intuition.) This process of collecting images allowed me to keep focused on my dream by savoring the images and information about my goals. I had no idea how I was going to get there; I only knew that one day I would.

Images bring us pleasure. We cannot underestimate the power of pleasure in creating and in making any change in your life sustainable. When we experience beauty, we feel pleasure. Beauty is not just something we see; it is something we feel. Again, we see the importance of feelings. It is about connecting to what matters to you and what is meaningful to you.

Your road to calm is cultivated by inviting beauty and pleasure into your daily life based on what matters most to you. When you anchor your life to the beauty of what is meaningful to you, the choices and decisions you make are quick, clear, and consistent. Enjoyment is necessary for creating new ideas and trying new practices.

Another way creative people get into making and executing their ideas is a process of *time-released brainstorming*. You might meet with a group of trusted friends to discuss an idea or problem, make a visual map or timeline, and then go away and let your intuitive unconscious take the lead as you relax in your hammock. Allow your thinking mind to just relax. Trust that something will arrive when you let things go. When you least expect it, a new idea emerges that might be the result of a combination of things. Neuroscience research into creativity has found that relaxation, pleasure, and distraction are the keys to allowing your subconscious mind to plant ideas into your conscious mind. That's the making process that leads to new thinking or innovation.

Earlier, I mentioned my hobby of painting. After an hour or so of painting, I take time to walk away from my artwork for a while and then come back with fresh eyes. This is a design thinking process: let go in order to arrive. Part of making is knowing when to rest your mind and allow your heart to speak.

Design Making in Action

I have learned to take this design thinking skill of doing and non-doing and apply it to my life. Many years ago I had two changes I wanted to implement. First, I wanted a career shift from health promotion to an entrepreneurial lifestyle business. Second, I wanted to live in a house rather than an apartment. I made a collage of my dream career from images and words cut from magazines. I filled the poster board with images and statements about the work I wanted to do and the global vision that I had for my work. I also created a folder of my dream house and again filled this binder with images and ideas about the home design, landscape, and community. All these items were visible and accessible for me to see as the days passed.

I began to take inspired action toward these goals and started planning the creation of a healthy care package company. Several months later I received a call from a colleague and faculty member in the University of Virginia provost's office. She told me there was a new job opening and that she thought I would be a great candidate. She encouraged me to apply. To top it off, she told me it came with a house. I was not expecting this opportunity. I was on the track of being an entrepreneur with a global perspective. The job was the Director of Studies for the

International Residential College at the University of Virginia. It was a newly established residential college and I would be involved in creating the programs, courses, and leadership programs for the students in this global living and learning community.

I applied for the job and before the interview I spent a few days reflecting by writing and creating a "happy at work" vision board filled with images and words that described my vision for my job at the International Residential College. (You'll find instructions for making one of your own in Chapter 5.) The morning of the interview I looked at my collage and, in a flash of intuition, decided to bring it to the interview. I wanted to be myself in the interview and show my process with the team. It was a risk, but one worth taking. I met with a group of faculty and students in the provost's office and shared my ideas and thoughts, using my collage as a visual support.

They enjoyed my presentation, and one of the faculty members asked if she could keep the collage. I gave it to her and left satisfied that I had been true to myself and had done my best. Shortly after getting the exciting call that I got the job and accepting the position, I was taken on a tour to look at my new home. It is a beautiful historic home that was built by Professor Emmett, the first natural history professor hired by Thomas Jefferson, the founder of the university.

The house is nestled in a historic arboretum, just a block away from my best friend Julie's house, in a beautiful neighborhood next to the university. I can't tell you how many times over the years of our friendship the thought came into my mind, *I wish I lived near Julie.*

I will admit I was as surprised as you may be that this had happened. No one could have planned a better next step for me. My teaching motto has always been, "Make a plan, but plan to break it." In my classroom I start with a plan, but if something comes up, I am ready to take a detour. The same is true with life. Sometimes our best plans will be interrupted as providence steps in to direct us toward something greater.

Taking some time in my hammock and using the practices in this book, my life has taken many unexpected and expanding turns. The process of using your imagination and making models for what you are envisioning in your life puts you into the creative process of refining your vision.

Once you are inspired, begin by taking some small, daily, and happy action steps to make some imagery that represents your life dream come alive. And at the same time, be open to something greater. Put your focus or mind's eye on the end result, not how you are going to get there. Your vision of the end result, along with inspired action and belief of the possible, enables you to design a life unique to you. More things will flow to you that create meaning and significance in your life.

Designing calm is about being intentional in your thoughts, words, and actions. Ideas can come from everywhere and anyone. See how slowing down allows you to be present, patient, and positive in your interactions with others. Look for the possibilities every day. In design making, we see the value these activities have in creating the *feelization,* which fuels motivation for action. Think about a time when you made something. We feel great value and ownership when we have the experience of making.

The design-making process includes:

- *Imagery:* Daydream, use visual reminders, and write an ideal scenario.

- *Generating ideas:* Sketch to think, mind-map, or share with a good listener.

- *Making objects:* Create collages and folders to help focus and expand ideas.

Now you are ready to take more specific action toward making a lifestyle of calm with design doing. In the next section, you will become more involved in taking practical action steps toward your vision.

The Third Element of Design: Doing

After you have completed the design-making process of working with your imagination by making collages, writing, and creating images of your desired outcome, you are ready to move into a different level of action. The third element of the design process is about taking real-life action by experimentation, feedback, and redoing. We all have health and wellness habits that need a little tweaking. Many of us continually start and stop new health regimes. With some patience and motivation, actions become so ingrained in our way of being that they don't seem like practices at all. Remember learning to brush your teeth? It was a health habit that in the beginning took reminders from a parent, praise from the dentist, tasty toothpaste, and your daily effort.

Creating a habit is a great way to anchor something into your lifestyle. As you begin to implement new ideas and lifestyle habits, I want you to think like a designer and just start somewhere. Take action. This is a starting point, not the "be-all and end-all." It is just the beginning. The design process of doing is about reiteration, trial and error, starts and stops. If something doesn't work, try, try again.

Many of us have done this in creating change in our lives. If I'd known about this self-forgiving design principle of doing, I could have relaxed more around my change process. Self-acceptance wrapped in compassion is the key to self-kindness that allows for greater ease in the change process. I want you to start and stop and find what works best for you. Think *presence,* not *progress* or *perfection.* Stay present as you play with the process. Presence allows for more opportunities in this step of taking action.

Have you ever made a mistake? Hooray for you. You are creative and making mistakes is part of the creative process of doing. Having a mistake-positive attitude is the key to learning, creativity, and innovation. As you continue on this journey of designing calm, you will have to embrace failure. Some of the practices I share might not work for you. This is about experimentation and having a playful attitude in developing your creative confidence.

Learning to Juggle

In my classroom, I demonstrate how to have a mistake-positive attitude through the process of teaching my students how to juggle. The first thing I teach is dropping and picking up the balls. When you are learning to juggle, you are going to make many mistakes. So we start there, getting comfortable with having a beginner's mind and making mistakes.

How many times have you not taken action because things were not perfect? That is why doing is important.

We can't wait for perfection to get our ideas out in the world. Doing allows us to put our ideas into action. That is how we learn.

I was inspired to teach my students juggling after hearing Michael Gelb speak at the Darden School of Business. He wrote the book *More Balls Than Hands: Juggling Your Way to Success by Learning to Love Your Mistakes* and was speaking to MBA students interested in entrepreneurship. This book has some great lessons on creating a mind-set for creative change by learning the lesson of how to juggle.

Before I could teach my students something, I needed to learn it myself. I'd secretly wanted to learn to juggle, so this was a great motivation for me to do so. I looked at many books and videos online, but Gelb's book was the most helpful. As I learned and made mistakes, I was able to take that lesson of humility to my students.

One of the central lessons in Gelb's book is about unconditional self-acceptance or self-kindness. We need to give ourselves kudos for doing and accept our mistakes as part of our path to progress. If we approach our doing with this mind-set, we can use the power of unconditional acceptance to see the current reality and still envision the future outcome. Then, this gap that holds the creative tension between the reality and goals is bridged with love.

There is tremendous power in self-acceptance, and that power is love.

Change requires pleasure, and a small, frequent, or daily ritual. I spent about 15 minutes a day practicing juggling. I dropped so many balls my legs were sore from squatting down to pick them up. Over time, my small, daily, and happy practice resulted in my first *juggulation*. I had taught myself how to juggle but, more important, I was able to share this process and mind-set with my students.

The Mind-Set of Doing

Have you ever wanted something and would not take no as an answer?

My hunch is you probably had the mind-set of doing. You kept to the task of doing as much as you could to make something happen. Like learning to ride a bike for the first time, there was strong motivation and a desire for pleasure. It is important to bring pleasure into the change process.

When I have interviewed people who made lifestyle changes, I always got the same answer: "I decided." They looked themselves in the eye and decided to do something different until they achieved the results they wanted. That is how you change. You decide, and you keep taking daily, consistent, inspired action.

Several years ago, I had a strong motivation to make something happen. Remember the great job I got that came with the historic house located in a beautiful arboretum?

Well, when I took a look at the house for the second time, I did not see the beauty of the house I originally viewed. This second visit I spent imagining myself in the house and having students and other faculty guests and visitors. I realized it needed some renovations. The kitchen was a mess with large blaring fluorescent lighting, the floor had old linoleum, the sink was tiny, and it lacked counter space. The bathroom was in similar disrepair, and the wood floors throughout the house were painted and in need of refinishing. The whole interior of the house was painted dirty white. I made a list and requested the renovations. I got an immediate "no."

So, I used design discovery and began to ask myself questions about the home and how it related to my work. I imagined and thought about how I would use the house for teaching and gatherings and decided to create a renovation notebook. Just like in the last section on design making, I pulled pictures of everything I wanted. After that, I quickly moved into design doing. I went to Lowe's and found paint colors for each room, new fixtures, tile, appliances, and everything else I needed. Then I wrote a list of what the new position was and how I would be using the house to host students and faculty. I resubmitted a new request with additional detailed information from my list regarding the beauty of the home and how it would be used to develop this new community.

My request was approved on a Thursday. They wanted me to pick out colors, fixtures, countertops, and appliances by Monday. Thank goodness I followed these three elements of design. By using the design elements of discovery, making, and doing, it was easy to respond quickly. I was at the house the day the painters came to paint the interior. They had been painting this house for years and had always painted it an off-white color throughout the home. They looked concerned and said, "If we paint it all these colors, it is going to make it difficult for the next person."

I explained that I understood in the past this house was used for visiting professors for a year and then the next one would move in. But, I assured them, I would be staying for a number of years. When I came back later in the day, they were beaming. The colors I chose for each room added elegance and enhanced the architecture of the house. The painters were so excited as we walked from room to room. It was as if they'd painted a masterpiece.

My message to you is to keep going, even if your ideas or plans don't look possible. Keep *doing*. You never know when what you make may come in handy at a later time.

Dealing with Doubt

The *doing* element can help with that voice in your head that likes to overthink. If you are like me you have gotten caught up with overthinking a problem or idea. Stress speaks to us in the language of fight, flight, freeze, or figure out. Most of us stay in our heads trying to figure things out, which stresses us even more. We overthink instead of jumping in and doing.

As an educator, my passion has always been to enhance the well-being of others. While working with a new habit or goal, I find every once in a while a doubt or worry creeps in my mind: *How will I get this done? What if no one signs up for the workshop?*

This can be show-stopping thinking. I have learned from experience to turn worry into an honest concern. Worry is something that wants to be heard. I prefer the word *concern*. A concern is something that can be eased with an action plan. Planning happens in the present moment, leaving worry in the dust. Any time you are worried, take some time in quiet, ask a question, make a plan, and take an action. Taking action in the present can dissolve the anxiety of a doubt, worry, or concern. Remember to be flexible. All change brings challenges and all challenges bring change. So it helps to have a tool to process your challenges.

Here's a simple design process for challenges:

- See the problem.

- Understand the challenge by gathering information. Ask questions.

- Focus on the solution or end result.

- Make it visual with a map, collage, or folder.

- Search for the meaning and generate ideas.

- Write in your notebook about possible outcomes and how to work around obstacles. Put it aside overnight.

- Let it go, and let inspiration arrive.

- In the morning, review with fresh eyes. Look for new questions.

- Take inspired action for the best result.

- Look to see if the changes bring results and then refine.

Creating change can be difficult and often comes with starts and stops. When you ask anyone about a significant change they have made in their lives, you will hear a story of struggle filled with speed bumps that slowed progress. For example, during my first year of college as an art major, I began smoking because all the artists smoked.

I guess I just wanted to fit in with the crowd. It was something to do while we took a break to step away from our paintings. This time of stepping away allowed us to come back with fresh eyes to our canvas.

Smoking was a ridiculous habit for a health nut to take up, and I quickly became addicted. I tried to quit 20 times over five years, trying a variety of methods: hypnosis, Nicorette gum, cold turkey, and so on. I even tried my own form of aversion therapy, which consisted of sitting in front of a mirror while smoking and telling myself how bad my hair smelled, how tired my body felt, and how disgusting I looked with a cigarette perched on my lips. None of these attempts worked. Then one day I woke up and declared I would never smoke again. That was it. Sure, the three weeks it took to detoxify were rough, but I had *no doubt about it*. Determination took hold.

"I decided" are the words of change.

For over five years, I had visualized myself healthy and breathing fully. I imagined myself more active and enjoying sports. After a while, I got a gym membership and supported my image with action by being around healthy role models. I changed my tribe and used the power of social programming to shift my thinking, beliefs, and action.

In hindsight, my failed attempts gave me new insights, ideas, and ways to design my way of quitting a bad habit. I needed something that worked for me, not one designed for the masses. My reiterations built the fortitude needed to end that battle. Never underestimate the value and momentum of small steps.

The Benefits of Design Doing

As an artist, I love the process of design and have used design tools in my personal development and coursework with my students. Thinking like a designer allows us to pay attention, suspend our judgment, use empathy, and expand our creativity. By using the design tools of inquiry, visualization, collaging, and journaling, among others, we can generate new insights and solutions and then use our rational mind to reflect and experiment.

The design process is what puts thinking into action. Design practices are enjoyable, doable, and effective in creating the change we desire in our lives. Design solves problems by exploring, experimenting, and tweaking solutions. The practices of design bring some compassion and happiness into the change process.

When we come from the mind-set of designing our life, we claim the power of turning our busy world into a world of beauty. The design process puts us in the state of flow where time slows down as we engage ourselves fully in being present. In fact, researchers have studied people who make crafts, like knitting, and found it is similar to a form of mindfulness meditation. Who knew knitting was creating the same calm brain waves as seen in a meditative breathing practice? Designers like the combination of effort, fun, and relaxation. They have a mind-set that allows for a balanced time for reflection, visualization, and inspired action.

I've noticed that my students show more willingness to take risks with new ideas when engaged in design thinking activities. They make stronger connections to the material because they are actively engaged. And they make stronger connections to each other working in collaboration as a team.

For example, on the first day of class I used to go through the syllabus by reading different sections out loud. After the first weeks of school, it was clear to me that this method was not working. Inevitably, students would come into class, week after week, with questions that were covered in the syllabus.

On the first day of class one year, I decided that my new class would break into small groups and draw the syllabus. This required brainstorming different ways to depict images as they worked in collaborative teams. They really had to read the syllabus, discuss, and draw images on extra-large paper taped on the walls. Though they initially moved through the process with apprehension, they were transformed by the state of being fully engaged.

Hesitation turned into excitement. The room was buzzing with energy and ideas.

This process allowed them to take risks with their designs. Afterward, we walked to each poster-size display; and they shared the process of how they talked, argued, and laughed over what pictures to use as they shared their understanding of what the class demands would be.

My students showed a higher level of joy, engagement, and collaborative learning while using this design process, and the activity introduced them to the beginning of how to think like a designer. They had to ask questions, think with images and symbols, work as a team, and discuss and share ideas. This activity immediately desensitized them to failure. They learned the first day of class to take a risk and to have a mistake-positive attitude.

The design-doing process includes:

- *Experimentation:* Give it a go, try something different.

- *Feedback:* Ask for help.

- *Reiteration:* Do a redo.

Experimentation brings your ideas to life. Feedback and reiteration are invaluable in developing your path to calm. Evaluate what feedback is relevant and examine how you can integrate that in your next steps toward a calm lifestyle. One of the living assignments I give my students is to spend the week *asking for help.* So many of us try to figure things out on our own. This isolation can lead to frustration and giving up. In my career I realized most people have difficulty asking for help. Thank goodness asking for help is a design skill of discovery. In work and in life, we are in many partnerships and teams. The skill of asking for help is important for successful collaboration.

At the end of the following chapters in this book, I offer suggestions on how to use these three elements of design—discover, make, do—to make it easier for you to practice calm. Let the designer's mind be your companion on the road to having more relaxation, mindfulness, and positivity in your life.

In the next chapter I will share how relaxation is the foundation to all behavior change and the foundation for resiliency. You will be introduced to the value that creating moments of relaxation has on your daily routine and on your ability to meet the challenges of the day. More relaxation equals more joy. When we are relaxed, we have the capacity to experience joy from others as well as cultivate ways to share more joy in our daily lives.

2

relaxation

DESIGNING JOY

My time in the hammock is a restorative practice, bringing me the kind of happiness that comes from deep relaxation. I love hanging out with this feeling of inner joy.

I found my way to sustainable ease and joy by creating a daily practice of just being. I enjoyed my practice of slowing down. It wasn't tied to a religion. I had no mantra. I didn't have to sit up straight with my legs crossed. There was no sense of seriousness, pressure, or stress of doing it right. My mind-set was not on *doing,* it was on just *being* and letting the body do its undoing. What I experienced was the natural balancing of the mind and body. It felt like the body's natural intelligence was at work. This is what I hope this book will help you find: inner peace.

We each have the innate power to heal our bodies and take control of our lives through the practices of relaxation, mindfulness, and positivity. These resourceful states create new brain-body patterns that over time become natural to our way of being. Undoing is doing something. It was my diligence and commitment to a daily practice of quiet that has improved my physical and mental wellness.

My hurried thinking became calmer. My sense of humor returned at a moment's notice. I take life's ups and downs less personally. Happiness for no apparent reason is my new normal. Just being in a state of deep appreciation improves my day. It is not a thinking state but a being state: the simple art of being present.

When we close our eyes, the body responds. We become slowly aware of the senses and the energy in the body. As you practice allowing, you may think you are doing nothing. What is happening is an unraveling of tension and strain. The body's natural intelligence is attending to the body's systems. You realize that your natural state is calm and resourceful. The body leads the mind to find the stillness naturally within. As thinking slows, we move more into our senses, feeling the body breathe. The mind and body let go and relax, and what seemed like a passive state is very active. I can feel my muscles soften. My breath takes on a greater presence, and I feel waves of energy move through me. Breathing makes the unconscious conscious.

The more I practiced, the more I understood my body's signals. I began to gain an understanding of how my body was communicating to me. It's as if the body says, "Thank you. You remember that I am here, too."

As you enter more into a receptive state, feel and know that this practice is all you need. I found a place where it was easy to let go of worries, fears, and regrets. My hammock practice left me with an experience that changed my life—an enjoyable practice of undoing. I experienced my physical pain diminish, my mental stories deconstruct, and my trust in honoring my intuitive solutions increase. After months of my hammock practice, my outerwear of flip-flops matched my inner sense of joy.

"Go Slow" Became My New Mantra

Simple, everyday, focused activity can be the solution to ease the busy, stressed-out life. You do not need a hammock but you do need to take moments of joy, relaxation, and quiet in your day. The practice of stillness counterbalances the stress responses of fight, flight, freeze, or a "figuring out" mind. We are inundated by choices and information. Much of our stress today is caused from overthinking things. We can't slow the world but we can be aware of the mind. We can direct our energy using positive intention and action to create a new habit of calm.

Today's research confirms that a quiet mind is healthy and strong. If you Google the terms *meditation* or *mindfulness,* you will see a trend in finding quiet and peace in our day-to-day routine. In fact, the company Google teaches their employees mindfulness skills for health and well-being. Many executives, parents, and students I have worked with, of all ages and backgrounds, are seeking the skills for well-being. They are looking for natural ways to practice the internal strategies of stillness, compassion, and positivity that lead to developing a calm, creative mind.

Consider the following questions. If you answer yes to any of them, then it's time to remake your lifestyle.

- *Have I ever felt overwhelmed with all the demands of life?*

- *Is the caffeine habit I use to keep up the fast pace of my life now zapping my energy?*

- *Are new ideas passing me by because stress has become a habit?*

There is a plethora of books on happiness. In fact, when I tried to order one to use as a text for my class—the title was out of stock. My students and I had a good laugh.

You can't buy happiness! I describe this external seeking to my college students by giving them the image of chasing a dog named Happy. Just when you get close enough to catch Happy, he's off and running. We are all endlessly chasing Happy.

For many years, I looked for external sources to help manage my stress, time, and schedule. I focused on resolving my symptoms of depression, excess weight, and back pain. I searched everywhere for answers and remedies. I looked for books, magazines, workshops, and seminars on stress management, time management, weight management, and lessons on how to *just say no*. My strategies appeared to work for a while, keeping stress at bay. Eventually, as the symptoms returned, I was off seeking another strategy, diet, or workshop. From reading the latest self-help books to meeting with professionals, my personal mantra remained steadfast: "What's wrong with me?"

Growing up, I was a chubby kid. According to our cultural ideals, I was flawed. I grew up believing I was fat and became a regular dieter and binge eater. It was the perfect relationship—one complemented the other. For years, my mental focus around food was skewed. I would go off and on diets, reinforcing my belief: *I can't lose weight.*

The more the focus was on restriction, the more it reinforced the belief of not being able to lose weight. Having developed a greater understanding of the nature of the mind, the biochemistry of the body, and nutrition, I began to understand how my nutrition beliefs, food sensitivities, overexercising, and poor sleeping habits were keeping me fat. I needed to relax. My weight naturally dropped when I was fully engaged with creative hobbies, activities, and friends that I loved. When I would spend weekends drawing and painting, my stress and weight decreased and my happiness increased. Painting put me in the flow state, where I was fully engaged and confident, and where time expanded. My hunch is many of us need to spend less time in the gym and more time on things that bring us excitement and joy.

I craved change and at the same time resisted it. It seems we all want more energy and fulfillment in life, yet when given models or opportunities for change, many of us resist it. Why? Because we are using outdated models for change that focus on the symptoms. We live in a culture of addictions where many of us are self-medicating with food, sex, alcohol, TV, computers, cell phones, and just keeping ourselves overly busy. With training in relaxation, mindfulness, and positivity, we can begin shifting toward balance and a mind-set that is creative.

Relaxation allows for old habits to unravel as we cultivate positive emotions and a meaningful direction for our lives. Relaxation can be the missing element in maintaining a healthy weight, and happiness comes from developing a calm mind where you can be fully connected to your feelings and to others.

If you are looking for increased freedom, a calm mind can be your ally. While the initial prerequisite to change is a sense of urgency, lasting change requires inner peace so that old beliefs that no longer serve us can drop away. Creating inner peace involves slowing down enough to befriend our emotions and use them as guidance. Once emotional intelligence is gained, we can think clearly and act decisively. Taking a holistic approach to health and self-development requires taking personal responsibility and action. But often we overthink, complicate, and move in the wrong direction, avoiding the basics of a healthy lifestyle.

If we want to improve the general quality of our lives, seeking happiness may not be the place to start. I think we need to start with relaxation to allow time for the body to process feelings and energy we have been exposed to throughout our day. Relaxation teaches us to be present with ourselves. When we *feel* active, secure, and connected, we are naturally happy. Joy is that feeling of connection to our mind, body, and spirit, and it begins with relaxation. To get to this feeling of joy, it helps to use a relaxation practice to process your feelings.

The Most Important Pose in Yoga: Deep Relaxation

One way people have tapped into learning about this quality of deep relaxation is through yoga. Yoga has become popular because it is a method that allows you to slow down, relax, and be present with your mind and body. Many of us have done yoga and experienced the benefits that breathing and stretching have on the mind and body. You come in exhausted from a long day and, like magic, by the end of class you're revived, relaxed, and energized. Yoga is an active practice that develops and strengthens our connection to the mind, body, and spirit. *Yoga* means "union": the combining of skills for the mind, body, and spirit to create balance.

Yoga is an excellent example of a practice that, with diligence, requires us to be present in the moment, focused, and aware. The most important pose of the series is the last pose, *savasana,* in which you are lying down on your back with your eyes closed in deep relaxation. In silence and stillness, yet awake with awareness, you let go of the day and revel in calmness. It is a simple pose composed of the brilliance of just being. During this practice of *savasana,* the brain enters a very open and stable place. This relaxation yoga pose is a simple introduction to practicing relaxation.

In savasana, the teacher guides you to relax the muscles in the body, letting go of the mental and physical strain of the day. After the movement practice of yoga that stretches the body, the final relaxation pose lets the mind relax and allows the body's intelligence to take over. As you let go, you arrive at your innate calmness and connection to your natural brilliance. A good yoga teacher will spend 15 to 30 minutes on this pose.

This final, powerful pose of deep relaxation is all we need to slow down and feel the connection we have with the energy of our body and spirit. If yoga isn't of interest, guided relaxation has great value in building a foundation of calm. Breathing fully and completely is also an important tool in creating a calm mind and relaxed body.

Relaxation has been studied for many years, and the research demonstrates its beneficial effects on the immune system and psychological well-being, which, in turn, move us closer to the ultimate state of creating personal joy. Relaxation helps restore and enhance the body systems for health, well-being, and resilience. Dr. Herbert Benson, who coined the term *relaxation response,* conducted research at Harvard Medical School that concluded: "The relaxation response–based approaches used in combination with nutrition, exercise, and other interventions resulted in the alleviation of many stress-related medical disorders."

Relaxation is a learned skill and can be practiced any-time and anywhere. Because of our fast-paced life, our time for stillness is limited. Many of us have lost the ca-pacity to relax and breathe deeply. The good news from neuroscience is the brain can change, and we can create new pathways of calmness that can override the old stress pathways of being frazzled. Taking frequent one-minute relaxation breaks throughout the day can create a habit of calm.

Breathing, a Simple Relaxation Tool

When I was a health educator, we would often take relaxation breaks in our office. One relaxation practice I used was what I called the "legs up on the wall" pose. I found a space in my office where I could lie down with my legs propped up against the wall. This is a great way to de-compress if you've been on your feet all day. It caught on in my office, and soon there were two or three of us doing the "legs up on the wall" pose for five-minute breaks. We started calling it the bat pose. Talk about joy! We were tapping into our joy center by taking the time to slow down and feel. It made the whole office calmer and more relaxed.

If you don't want to get down on the floor, you can just do some gentle breathing and slow stretching in what-ever way feels comfortable to you. When stress becomes a habit, it causes us to hold our breath or keep it very shallow, breathing from our upper chest. Many of us sit all day and do not take the time to move our body. Creating several breathing and stretching routines throughout the day can release built-up strain in our bodies. Taking the time to replenish yourself with breathing and stretching can bring some relief and build resiliency as you move through your day.

The cornerstone to managing your energy is learning to relax. Peacefulness, inner stillness, starts with relaxation. Stretching and breathing practices are the mind-body science of relaxation. As we allow the body and mind to relax, the mind's power to direct attention is harnessed. This training in relaxation is similar to what actors, musicians, high-performance athletes, and practitioners of martial arts have studied for years. When we extend our mental and physical energy, we need time to integrate and recover. Relaxation brings renewal and energy. We know that a relaxation practice brings us into calmness, and calmness is power. The single most important tool is the breath. The breath helps us to relax. Learning some basic breathing skills will bring enhanced results for relaxing the body and developing a quiet mind. We can't think our way to calm; we need to breathe and feel our way to calm.

Breathing consciously creates more oxygen that equates to more power. The body works most efficiently with the energy of oxygen. We have developed habits of breathing based on our frantic patterns of stress. These short, shallow breaths we take can keep us locked into the stress pattern. Learning deep breathing exercises is practical because once you learn them, then you can use these tools to center yourself anywhere.

The immediate benefits of these breathing practices are many: They clear the mind of chatter, reduce cravings, and, as you practice, the breath becomes even and stable, leading to a balanced nervous system and allowing the body to relax. The long-range benefits include greater emotional control, increased perceptual sensitivity, and increased mental clarity.

When I teach relaxation, I always begin with the breath. Breathing brings us into the here and now. We can all handle the present moment. It's the past and future that get us frazzled. A beginning relaxation tool is paying attention to the breath. When we focus on the breath, it does two things. It connects us to our bodies and brings us mentally into the present.

An MBA student I worked with reported, "You changed my life. My husband did not recognize me. I was so relaxed when I came home. I always thought I was an anxious person. Now I know I can be calm." We all can be calm. Living well is living skillfully and compassionately with the struggles in the moment versus chasing the Holy Grail of happiness. It is so much easier to move through life with the grace of an open heart. As our ability to relax, observe, and inquire within develops, we replace old patterns and experience more freedom.

Relaxation has a powerful effect on our biology, brain, and brilliance. The brain controls our immune system through the vagus nerve. It is one of the most important nerves coming from the brain as it travels to all the major organs. Through relaxation, you activate the vagus nerve and affect your immune cells, reduce inflammation, and prevent stress-related disease. Scientists have studied brain states of calm for years, learning that relaxation, a state of calm, peace, and stillness, activates the vagus nerve to enhance health. We experience more joy when we are relaxed enough to be available to the wonders of our daily lives.

Do you have some wonderful memories that to this day always relax you? Recalling such experiences can assist you to sink deeper into a state of calm. Our memories of relaxation are a useful tool in training the body to relax. Some common memories include summer vacations or holidays with friends, watching the water, basking in the sun like a lazy cat, being in nature, or just laughing with family and friends over a home-cooked meal. We all have a go-to place in our mind where we can recall and imagine the feelings, sensations, and qualities of calm.

Relaxation is easier when we have established health habits that promote calm. The basic relaxation lifestyle habits are to eat real food, drink water, and get a good night's sleep. It seems the number one complaint I hear from students and clients is the lack of sleep. Learning to relax is a great beginning in establishing a routine. I discuss this with my students on the first day of class. You can use the practices in this book to help you hone these core lifestyle habits. Look for ideas and practices in Chapter 5.

Relaxation is like the white space in a painting or graphic design. It is necessary. The white space is doing something—creating balance. Balance is a key part of designing calm. We need the excitement of life as well as the calm time. Balance allows for sustainable happiness.

Living in a state of health and well-being makes your life easier. We learned in this chapter how taking small moments of relaxation throughout your day is restorative. We often do not have the time for a long meditation or even a nap. Yet a minute here and there throughout the day can make a big impact on your energy and well-being. Relaxation is the first step to designing calm.

In the next chapter, you will discover the secret to changing your patterns of negative thinking with compassion and presence: *mindfulness*. This is the second aspect to designing calm in your life. Mindfulness hones your awareness and compassion, the two elements needed to change your relationship to stress. While we can't get rid of all stress, we *can* change our relationship to it. Changing a lifestyle habit can be stressful. We need awareness and self-compassion in the rocky change process. It's a trial-and-error road, so self-forgiveness is key.

How do you want to show up in the world? What habits do you need to cultivate to be more joyful, compassionate, and brilliant? Think about one keystone lifestyle habit you would like to change as you read the chapter on mindfulness. A keystone habit is a lifestyle habit that has a domino effect on other habits in your life. For example, when I get a good night's sleep (keystone), I have more self-kindness and energy to exercise and more clarity to choose healthy foods. The bottom line in cultivating compassion is taking care of oneself. From this place of self-kindness and well-being, you can extend compassion and kindness to others.

Discover|Make|Do
use relaxation to design joy in your day

- **Discover** what places, people, and spaces make you feel relaxed.

- **Make** a practice of smile breathing throughout your day. (See Chapter 5.)

- **Do** 5 to 15 minutes of hammocking or deep relaxation.

3

mindfulness

DESIGNING COMPASSION

Mindfulness is the cultivation of awareness, acceptance, and compassion. In explaining this concept to my students, I draw the two wings of mindfulness—awareness and acceptance—and I place compassion in the middle. Compassion means the desire to alleviate suffering. You can begin expressing it with yourself, then extending it to those around you.

When people work with a positive mind-set, performance on nearly every level—productivity, creativity, communication—improves. Designing a calm, positive mind-set begins with the self-compassion that comes from mindfulness. Research from various scientific and health-related fields shows us the value that calm has on

49

our overall well-being. Developing a quiet mind is more than positive thinking; it is about understanding the nature of the mind-body connection, developing a new relationship with stress, and cultivating qualities that support well-being. When we change our relationship to stress and let go of our worries by focusing on solutions, our mental landscape becomes calm and receptive. We are cultivating compassion in discovering our mental habits with observation, acceptance, and kindness. This is how we change, with love.

"Mindfulness is beautiful and nerve-racking, too," one of my students shared in class.

It is true that mindfulness does not equate to relaxation. Mindfulness and relaxation are different. Mindfulness has a focus on acceptance, even if it feels uncomfortable. While we can become relaxed while practicing mindfulness, it is simply about being present in the moment without judgment. It is noticing our various feelings, thoughts, and sensations. Yes, at first this can be nerve-racking until it becomes a gentle and kind way to be curious, open, and responsive rather than reactive. That is why the element of compassion is so important to developing self-kindness. When we get to the point of observing our thoughts and feelings as temporary, not facts, we can settle more into the moment. Learning the transient nature of thoughts and feelings can remove the worry and other unnecessary stressors.

At work, as soon as I feel fear, I let myself observe the tension with acceptance. This mindfulness process is the beginning of being able to reflect and respond effectively in work situations. The calm mind is peaceful, positive, and open to possibilities that make change possible. As one of my students stated, "It's all good." I loved her bright attitude and openness to observe without judging.

So when I get in a worried state of mind, I quietly begin to notice the mind and the stories. I begin with acceptance. I observe thoughts, feelings, and emotions in a noncritical way and then I question them. Are they true, or are they a story I made up in my head? I look at the concerns and ask myself, *What is it I am afraid of? Is there an action I can take?* This simple mindfulness practice of awareness, acceptance, and compassion quickly moves me back to a place of clarity and calm. It's not easy being human, but we don't have to make it harder than it needs to be. It took me a while not to take everything so personally. I worried about what others thought, and I wanted everyone to be happy.

The Body Does Not Lie

I was in my late 20s when I learned that a little kindness to myself can go a long way. Standing up for yourself doesn't have to be as frightening for you as it was for me at that age. Let me tell you a story.

I was gasping for air—a few minutes earlier, I had been called to the executive director's office of the large hospital where I was working. Seated across from me was the gruff, dark-suited CEO glued to his soft brown leather chair. He leaned forward over his mahogany desk and got right to the point as he firmly requested that I take on additional work. As I sat and listened, I felt a wave of dread run through my body. I opened my mouth to speak, but what came out was a gasp for air and then another. The sound from my throat grew louder as I struggled to breathe. Dread turned to fear.

As I struggled to breathe, our eyes met again. At this moment, his expression began to soften with concern. My direct supervisor, a cheery man, was also in the room. He handled the situation with ease and helped me regain my breath.

I did not have to take on the additional work that day. I was already stressed from a full workload, and my extreme stress response spoke louder than my words. That was my first and last experience with hyperventilating.

This incident heightened my quest for balance. I was already teaching relaxation, jogging, and taking an occasional yoga class. I had taken workshops on the mind-body connection. But the body does not lie; it was at this moment I realized there was something missing.

Later in my career, after years of studying mindfulness, I found greater ease in standing up for myself with co-workers and supervisors. I remember a time where I had to say no to a request for additional work. I found I was able to do so with ease. This time I asked my supervisor, "What would you like me to give up in order to take on this new project?" This communication opened the doors for greater clarity in the work process.

Minding the Pain

My mindfulness practice helped me process my emotions and provided the clarity I needed for business decisions. One area I had not used mindfulness for was to address physical pain. I knew from my research that mindfulness programs have been successfully used in hospitals for people with chronic pain.

Several years ago, I had a stubborn back pain that would not go away. It came one day and never left. I tried the usual home solutions, including stretching, hot compressions, resting, and walking. Later, I paid for the best alternative medical solutions, including massage, acupuncture, physical therapy, and osteopathy. I had seen all the top healers in my town over a period of a year with no resolution.

I decided to make an appointment with surgeons, two Army buddies ready to release me from my agony. They reviewed my MRI and said, "We can certainly do surgery. We have seen this before." One of them stated, "My wife has the same thing; sometimes she has pain and sometimes she does not." He had no explanation why one person would have pain and another would not.

"Sometimes she does not" stuck in my mind. I thanked the surgeons and told them I decided to put off the surgery. I went home with the mantra on my mind, *sometimes she does not,* and tried one more remedy: mindfulness. I knew that mindfulness is used with chronic pain patients in the hospital, so why not give it a try? I had never thought to use my mindfulness practice for pain. Every day for 15 minutes, I would lie in bed with my legs propped up on pillows and just breathe and watch with compassion and acceptance.

This was the first time I allowed myself to fully experience the pain. Acceptance was new. In the past, my goal was to get rid of the pain. Choosing acceptance was a new experience, and what I observed fascinated me. The sensation got big, then it got small, then big again. It moved to the right and left. I watched and allowed myself to feel it dance around me. My relationship with the pain changed. Instead of hating it, I held it in the arms of compassion. I developed a friendly relationship with my back, and we met daily for weeks until the pain was completely gone—and it has never come back.

Since then, I have heard many stories of people who were suffering and used mindfulness as a means to transform and heal themselves. It is a simple practice that requires stillness, attention, compassion, and acceptance. Mindfulness or a compassion practice can be incorporated into your daily routine. It is the one thing that can change your life. Consider this: What if you drop into your body and listen?

Running on Autopilot

Many of us are running on automatic pilot, unaware of what we are thinking or feeling. Ask yourself these questions. If you answer yes to any of them, then you may want to make mindfulness a daily practice in your life.

- *Have I ever found myself driving home and missing my exit?*

- *Do I have a rote answer when someone asks how I am?*

- *Do I often consume my meals without tasting them?*

- *Am I running on caffeine because that is my norm?*

- *Have I fallen into the trap of negative or worst-case-scenario thinking?*

When I realized I was allowing myself to run on automatic pilot, I saw I was not embracing my full potential. We have all developed habits of thinking and feeling, stories we tell ourselves beyond what is given at the moment. These may be cultural or family stories we grew up with. We tend to believe our stories because we have attached so much emotion to them.

Here are simple instructions for how to pay attention with mindfulness:

- Shift the way you see the pain and lean into it; feel it fully with kindness.

- Instead of blaming or avoiding, choose to stay present with your feelings.

- Let go of the thinking or the story you made up. Stay with the feeling.

Getting quiet builds the muscle of discernment. This begins with discovering the connection between your thoughts, feeling, and behaviors and how it affects your time at work and home. Increased awareness through creating a daily discipline of a mindfulness practice can help break the cycle of stress reactivity and allows a more centered state anytime and anywhere.

Mindfulness is a method of filtering information with our power of observations, allowing us to navigate toward what is right for us. Our critical thinking skills are enhanced when we hone the power to be present. When we live in the past rather than in the present, we miss the possibilities right in front of us.

Mindfulness at Work

Many times, I have used mindfulness in a difficult work situation to decrease stress and save time. For example, I had a new colleague from Yale who had all kinds of ideas for our student community. I felt my body tighten up as he talked about his plans. After the meeting, I sat in my office and reflected on my thoughts, feelings, and emotions. I watched my thoughts go from calling friends or my boss to complain, to having awareness of my insecurity of working next to a Yale-trained professor. When I stayed with the feeling of insecurity and experienced it with acceptance, all the drama dissolved.

This is an example of what we call the "monkey mind," where the brain is jumping all over the place, making up stories. Sitting there with all my thoughts and feelings was not comfortable, but I quickly moved through them, accepting my insecurity and my intuition. At the end of this mindfulness process, I felt complete. I did nothing. There was no drama. I realized my ego had been getting in the way. Even though my intuition and expertise thought the proposed programs would not work, what's the harm in trying out new ideas with our students? Playing with ideas, programs, and ways of doing things is simply part of the creative process. Mindfulness training allows people the opportunity to be more accepting, generous, and collaborative as things at home or within organizations change.

Mindfulness trains us to slow down, get quiet, and better see our mental and emotional patterns clearly with self-compassion. We see the monkey mind for what it is: fleeting thoughts. It was perfectly fine to be insecure about my Yale colleague.

Got drama going on in your head? Dissolve it with the self-kindness of compassion. Mindfulness is an ongoing process that is honed with openness and curiosity. Practice helps us see the monkey mind for what it is. Then we are able to respond effectively rather than automatically.

Mindfulness also supports the new focus on single-tasking work projects. Getting away from digital distractions that demand our attention and practicing single tasking can improve your work. Do you need to read something for work? Practice mindful reading, taking the time to absorb the text and allow the mind to reflect on the information.

Change Your Relationship to Stress

Most people think meditation is about stopping thoughts, getting rid of emotions, or controlling the mind, but it is actually about noticing the mind and stepping back to observe the thoughts and feelings clearly and without judgment. This requires a relaxed and focused mind.

We are creatures of mental, emotional, and physical habits. Habituated, we tend to think, feel, act, and speak the same patterns over and again. The patterns of our thoughts and emotions become our unconscious tap dance, the driving force for what we create in our lives. Our habits can also be called mental models, our ways of thinking, our beliefs, and our ideas of who we are in the world.

What are some of your habits of thinking?

One way to cultivate mindfulness is to be aware of times when you go on autopilot. We do it all the time, and this is a fun practice to move your attention gently. A mindfulness practice I use is to give my full attention to brushing my teeth. As part of your awareness training, try giving your full attention to a daily health activity. As you increase your attention, a natural result is an increase in wonder. Mindfulness is relational. It leads us to develop a relationship with ourselves. As we bring the qualities of awareness and compassion to ourselves, we can ease into acceptance of all our feelings. Instead of trying to get rid of stress, we change our relationship to stress.

You Can't Get Mindfulness Wrong

Our brains are active, and sometimes we just over-think things. Mental activity is not a sign of failure. A wandering mind is healthy and necessary in relaxation. In mindfulness practice, we continue to bring our aware-ness to the present by becoming aware and redirecting. If your mind is going to wander, you might as well let it wander in a positive direction.

A happy mind-wandering practice can be part of your hammocking relaxation practice. With mindfulness practice, we are noticing our automatic-pilot state and tethering ourselves back to the present. Taking time to acknowledge our mental and emotional landscape with self-compassion is acceptance. The key is not to run from uncomfortable feelings while also not indulging in them. With practice, we notice the quiet spaces between the thoughts and feelings.

Our attitude, how we pay attention with compassion, is essential. Think of self-compassion as a friend. Notice how thoughts become stories in our mind and how they can create emotion until, before we know it, we are emo-tionally hijacked. In shifting to awareness, we observe. We are not attempting to stop thoughts or feelings; we simply notice habits of thinking. We are cultivating a different relationship with thoughts and emotions. Compassion is the cornerstone of mindfulness.

Remember, our thoughts are habits. As you stay with the process of unconditional compassionate awareness, you will find a natural transformational process occurring. Compassionate self-awareness creates acceptance. Acceptance is simply being with what one is observing with kindness. As we look with self-compassion at our habits, the reactive patterns naturally unravel. We can embrace our flaws as beautiful imperfections. This is the core element of the *wabi sabi* mind-set. Wabi sabi is the Japanese art of appreciating the beauty of imperfection; everything is accepted as having some beauty. Through mindfulness, we focus on cultivating wholesome thoughts that support acceptance and well-being.

I believe mindfulness opens the door to forgiveness. Forgiveness is a powerful act that is healing not only for others, but also for you. We come to look at our thoughts and feelings with the lens of wabi sabi, accepting and appreciating it all. Everything is welcome, including sorrow or discomfort. This is the wise use of discernment in action. We can't truly create calmness if we are harboring anger toward another. Mindfulness supports being with the anger by bringing the darkness to the light of awareness where we can learn from our mistakes and come to understand the part we played. From this vantage point, we show up with a greater humility in our life's interactions.

I remember feeling furious with a co-worker. I went home and just needed to feel the anger, stomp my feet, and shout. I got the anger out of my body. Then I reflected and reviewed my perception of the situation. This process helped me release the anger and let go of any resentment. When we continue to direct ourselves to the present moment, we step into a place of power, possibility, and choice.

Here's how to use mindfulness in stressful situations:

- Practice acceptance and kindness toward your feelings of stress.

- Notice your thoughts of stress and the feelings of your upset.

- Go into the feeling and feel the sensations in your body.

- Calm yourself with your breathing.

- If needed, share your feeling with others clearly.

Mindfulness-based stress-reduction (MBSR) programs have been utilized in hospitals across the country for over 20 years. These programs have been found effective not only in reducing stress but also in reducing pain. In the past five years, these programs have been springing up in elementary and secondary schools, military training, prisons, juvenile detention centers, and executive development programs. Mindfulness training has a long history of evidence-based research, starting with the ground breaking work of Jon Kabat-Zinn. That speaks to the transformative power of the practice. Reading this book is the first step, and then playing with the practices with a group or on your own builds the qualities of curiosity, creativity, and connection we all love.

Compassion Is the Great Transformer

When we bring our attention, acceptance, and kindness to our feelings or our difficulties, we are building compassion. In life, we all have trials and tribulations, we often extend our suffering through our worry or ruminations. If we have some training of the mind, we become aware and fully present, letting go of worry. As we develop mindfulness, we see it is not only a training of the mind but also a training of the heart as our compassion expands.

We have to say yes to every moment we meet, even the ones we don't like. This is where the rubber meets the road in real-life situations. When you are facing a stressful situation, you can fight—or be curious. If you choose curiosity, you might ask, "What is this person showing me at this moment?" The answer will allow you to be more open and understanding to this person's struggle. Shine the light of awareness as a mirror to find your vulnerabilities. In this way, compassion for self and compassion for others deepens. If we say "yes" and "thank you" to the moment, it transforms us. Practicing compassion can help you see the value kindness can have in your work and life.

Find Your Mindfulness Tribe

Lastly, I would suggest you find a local mindfulness program and get support in training the mind to develop calmness in chaos. A group can support and assist you as you develop your practice. You will find a tribe of people who have compassion as the heart of their lives.

➤

The next chapter introduces you to the third and final element of designing calm: positivity and your inner brilliance. When we have taken the time to relax and be mindful, our inner whisperings of wisdom naturally gets louder. Our brilliance comes from using both our intellect and our intuition. The next chapter emphasizes the value positivity has on our day-to-day interactions for creating more value and meaning in our lives.

DISCOVER|MAKE|DO
use mindfulness to design compassion in your day

- **Discover** how you can bring the power of observation and kindness into your day.

- **Make** a "good day" mind map. (See Chapter 5.)

- **Do** fall asleep with memories of gratitude from your day.

positivity

DESIGNING BRILLIANCE

The third and last element of designing calm is positivity. By relaxing and listening deeply, we welcome our inner brilliance. The ability to reflect opens us up to our intuition and positive solutions. When we are calm and quiet enough to listen to our inner guidance, we are in tune with brilliance. Intuition is the flashes of insights we hear when we are relaxed, calm, and happy.

Brilliance Is Your Intuition Balanced with Your Intellect

The distractions of our world often keep us from listening to ourselves. Instead, we listen to others and ignore our inner wisdom. Your brilliance comes from slowing down enough to hear that calm inner voice of knowing and wisdom.

Once you get a message, do you follow it?

Brilliance is taking time to reflect on listening to that inner voice and then using your intellect to take the right action with confidence. It is a way of being in the flow of life with ease, knowing, trust, and grace. This is the final key in designing calm in your busy life.

The Voice of Intuition Is Clear, Concise, and Calm

In my late 20s, I was living in the middle of Wisconsin, working in a small town as a crisis counselor. My new co-worker, Fariba, was a graduate student studying dreams. One day she asked me if I wanted to take a road trip to Charlottesville, Virginia, for the International Dream Conference. I happened to have an old friend living in the town, so we loaded up the car and made our way to Virginia. We packed the car with all her healthy vegetarian food and took off driving for 13 hours, occasionally stopping to do some yoga or tai chi. We arrived, and I was enamored with the beauty of the University of Virginia and the surrounding Blue Ridge Mountains. My intuition hit me hard. The message was so clear, calm, and loud. I had to write it in my journal:

I am living in Charlottesville, Virginia.
I am working for the Office of Health Promotion.

It was such a strong, visceral feeling. I had a compelling inner voice settle in my mind. This intention anchored with my intuition.

I had never been so clear and concise on a life plan. Listening to my intuition, my inner brilliance, over the years I became familiar the quality of these powerful messages. My intuition comes swiftly, strongly, calmly, and clearly. I had a deep inner feeling of knowing I was meant to live in Charlottesville. Everything in my body said yes.

Immediately at the conference, I began meeting people, collecting business cards, and asking about work, even when people said there were no jobs and that the market was saturated with university graduates. Their sense of no did not diminish my inner sense of yes. Back at home I made a folder and filled it with pictures, cards, and articles about Charlottesville. Any time I saw a magazine article about Charlottesville or Virginia, I put it in my folder. A year went by and I had moved to a bigger city, Madison, Wisconsin. I still had my folder and daydreamed about Charlottesville. I often took time relaxing and breezed through my folder, imagining myself there. This time of reflection was powerful.

One day I got a strong intuitive hit that instructed, "Go to the library and look for a job in Charlottesville." I listened to my brilliance, went to the Madison Public Library, and looked in the East Coast papers. To my surprise, there was my job—sort of. I found a listing for a job as an alcohol and drug counselor at a hospital in New Hampshire with a sister facility in Charlottesville.

I called the facility to see if they had any openings in Charlottesville, but they said the only openings were in New Hampshire. I did not know anything about alcohol and drug counseling, but I applied anyway and studied for the position. Determined, I paid for my flight, aced the interview, and got the job. In my mind, however, I thought I would work there for a year and then transfer to Charlottesville.

I tell my friends that I took the long way to my goal. After a great year of working in New Hampshire, the hospital posted a job opening in Charlottesville. I got the job, moved, and immediately walked the grounds of the university. I stopped by the Office of Health Promotion and met the staff. No job openings.

About a year later, I got another intuitive hit: "Go to the Sierra Club picnic and go alone." (Do you ever argue with your intuitive brilliance? I do.)

Why? I thought. *Do I have to go? I don't want to go.*

"*Go,*" the voice said.

So I went and I met someone at the picnic from the University of Virginia's Student Health, who told me there was a job opening in Health Promotion. I applied and got the job. It was a part-time, temporary staff position, but I didn't care. As I walked to work across the famous Lawn at the University of Virginia, I felt the awe of abiding grace. Within a year, my job was a full-time faculty position. Brilliance is this type of fearless positivity in action. Having a clear intention, taking inspired action, and letting go of the outcome builds the mental muscle of positivity. It comes with practice. The more you pay attention to your intuition, the more positivity is cultivated in your mind and your life.

So many times, my intuition has guided me in the right path at exactly the right time. Did you notice nothing happened according to my timeline? I learned so much as an alcohol and drug counselor that if I had to do it again, I would take the same path. The joy and compassion you cultivate sustains you for the patience required to achieve your life's plan.

Brilliance Is Our Intuition Married with Discernment

Intuition comes in a flash and is fast, clear, and unemotional. Use your discernment on how to respond to your intuition.

Thoreau wrote that we discover new ideas, "like falling meteors," suddenly appearing before us "with a flash and an explosion." Cultivating the qualities of relaxation, mindfulness, and positivity builds your ability to be receptive, perceptive, and open.

One way to listen to your intuition is to ask your mind a question. Questions invoke curiosity. Your mind loves direction, so give it a positive question to solve.

What If Nothing Is Wrong with Me?

Many years ago, a friend invited me to a free self-development seminar. In our session, we wrote down the three things we wanted to change in our lives. Mine focused on career, romance, and a healthy weight. We all made our lists and, in the end, signed up to take the workshop that cost hundreds of dollars. I went home that night in a funk. *Haven't I done enough of these self-help workshops?* I thought.

I lay down on my bed and kept repeating, *What's wrong with me?*

Over and over, I repeated the question. Then a new question appeared: *What if nothing is wrong with me?*

As soon as I took in the freedom that came with this new question, I felt an electric current run through my body.

I thought to myself, *What if after all this time there is nothing wrong with me?*

It seemed at this moment everything changed for me. The next day my interactions seemed different. Men at the gym smiled at me and said hello. Everything seemed brighter. That night, I got a call from the workshop company saying they got my credit-card information wrong and needed the correct information to sign me up for the course.

I laughed and said, "I no longer need the course. I had my breakthrough by simply taking some time in quiet and allowing a different question to emerge."

Investigation of our thoughts is a positivity practice. I think I stumbled onto this positive practice of creating a new story when I asked the question over and over, "What's wrong with me?" and then I got the new question, "What if *nothing* is wrong with me?"

When we take time in stillness and reflection, we can see our thoughts clearly and begin to ask new questions. Be curious. Einstein was known for taking time to relax by sitting on the porch or enjoying his daily amble. He was a question-asker. His questions gave his mind a direction. The mind loves questions. During his relaxation time, he wasn't thinking about the answer. He let his mind relax and wander. The inner workings of the mind were making connections during this time of rest. Here is where the insights appeared. This is the brilliance process: getting quiet and calm, letting go of thinking, and allowing a being-state that supports insights and intuition to emerge.

Take a Brain Break

Educators know the brain needs breaks for learning. When taking in new information, it is important to take a break. This gives the brain time to make connections with the new information and create new insights. We all need to take some time to slow down and create calm in our lives.

While you relax and decompress, your brain has a chance to link the new information to old information, perhaps making some interesting and unexpected connections. When you find yourself in a cycle, stuck and looking for answers, go do something different. Sometimes we can't shift our thinking so we need to shift our body to allow new insights to emerge. Try going for a walk, contacting a friend, or making a cup of tea, in order to shift your energy and thinking. Use your mindfulness practice to slow down and get present and curious. Open yourself up to creativity, where failure is part of learning. Mindfulness is a tool that hones your emotional intelligence, the ability to regulate your emotions and respond effectively in life. One of my students put it simply, "Mindfulness is a time-saver and a mood lifter."

There is great value in the science of positive psychology that can help you develop your brilliance. Positive psychology focuses on studying the positive emotions that create well-being and meaning in our lives. Cultivating the skills that direct our mind supports us in creating calmness and creativity in our daily lives. We can use a gratitude practice to build positive emotions as well as hone our mindfulness toward gratitude. Look at the story you are telling yourself. See if you can see it from a different perspective. Psychologists have found this process of reframing beneficial in helping people see their life with new eyes.

Get Intentional

Another valuable positivity process is creating intentions to guide your day. Intention can be a powerful tool for harnessing the brilliance of your intuition. I love to create an intention as an anchor for my day or for a meeting.

I often reflect on my intention as I head into a meeting. Years ago I had the opportunity to teach a mindfulness leadership class in the Commerce School at the University of Virginia. I remember walking over to my first meeting with the dean of the school. I thought about him and his important and busy job and tight schedule. As I reflected on the meeting, I thought, *What do I want to happen at this first meeting?* Immediately my intuition replied, *I want to make a connection.* I imagined a relaxed and engaging conversation. I did not think how that was going to happen, and trusted my intuition. The essential feeling was *I want to make his day.*

When I got to the meeting, I met a very tall, serious-looking man. He was obviously busy and booked solid for the day. We sat down and began our talk. I noticed his stern eyes and serious demeanor, but as the conversation continued, he relaxed and was soon laughing. I believe having an intention to "make his day" directed my thinking and contribution to the conversation. When you set an intention, it is helpful to set it with an attitude of pleasure, well-being, or happiness. This process of an intention aligned with well-being provides direction to the mind and creates a feeling of ease. Directing your mind with positivity enhances your ability to perceive and make easy and quick decisions.

There are many ways we can use the science of the positive in our daily lives that build this quality of well-being. Martin Seligman, one of the founding fathers of positive psychology, has a classic assignment called "beautiful day." (You can find a version of it in Chapter 5.)

I give this assignment to my students. Essentially, it is taking some time to intentionally plan aspects of your day to make it beautiful. I ask my students to use the school day so they can see how a typical day can become extraordinary. They start by making an hour-by-hour plan, incorporating activities and people that they feel will bring feelings of joy into their day. For example, they may pay closer attention to the foods they are eating and with whom and how they are spending their time. They might add listening to music or going to a movie with a friend. The day is precious, so they want to be thoughtful and intentional about each moment. Some of the students' days work out perfectly; others do not.

My students and I have learned a lot about how our mind-set can make or break our day. Some students come in and say, "It rained on my beautiful day, so I picked another day." Other students understand that even when it rains, they can still have a beautiful day. You can choose if the weather is going to dictate your mind-set or not. Many of my students realize you can't plan a beautiful day with the expectation of perfection; life gets in the way, and many circumstances cannot be anticipated.

They do come to understand that how we accept and respond to our feelings, thoughts, and emotions can make all the difference in understanding that beauty is an inner quality. We can intend all kinds of affirmations for a beautiful day, but if we are not flexible to the uncertainty in life, we will suffer. Many of us needlessly suffer by thinking that things should be different. If we can practice acceptance, we immediately open up new possibilities and our anxieties or worries diminish. Once again, we see how a mindfulness practice enhances our ability to be a designer and be flexible in our daily lives.

Constraints Bring Creativity

Designers have constraints too when they work on a project. They would not say, "It's raining so I guess we should give up." No, they would take in the rain, observe it, feel it, and say, "What can I do with this rain?" The rain becomes part of the design of the day. It is not about perfection or process. It is about presence. Being present to the moment with full acceptance can lead to a beautiful rainy day. The presence of observing, accepting, and redefining or redesigning is the key to making each day beautiful.

Ask yourself: *What is this day showing me that I can view as positive?*

Maybe it is to slow down in order to appreciate the rain and the nurturing elements it has for us. Beauty can be found in the uncomfortable. We may need to readjust, rethink, and take a different action, like get a raincoat or enjoy an inside activity, to find the beauty. Many people miss the opportunity to transform their day from mundane to miraculous. I am an active person and love being outside. Rain does not disappoint me. I get excited when it rains because then I can go indoors and paint, write, or clean some clutter. I love how rainy days invite me to go inside to play. A practice of positivity can support a mind-set that is flexible and intuitive.

Right now I am using the analogy of a beautiful day, but it could be any life situation or personal interaction. We have all had interactions with people in our lives—family, friends, and co-workers—who can walk into a room stormy or sunny. Like the weather, other people's moods affect us. If someone bounces into the room with energy and a big smile, it is contagious. The same is true if you talk with a Debbie Downer (sorry, Debbie): We feel drained. Use your inner brilliance to guide you through a beautiful day regardless of the circumstances or the people you meet.

There are many ways your intuition can support your day. While writing this book, I got into the habit of eating chocolate. Granted, it was the very best dark chocolate. I researched two brands that had bars of 80 percent cacao, low-sugar dark chocolate. Everything was going along fine until I realized I was not eating just one square. I was eating half a bar. That was ten squares! In addition to the increase, I noticed it made me a little hyper. Since I was writing a book about calm, this was a contradiction. I decided I wanted to write the best book possible, and this meant no caffeine buzz.

My intuition kept saying, "Give up chocolate."

I resisted for a few weeks because I love chocolate, and I wondered how this would be possible. I have changed many habits in my life, and I know there are stops and starts. I felt I wanted to give up chocolate quickly and shorten the ups and downs of the process.

I talked to one nutritionist friend about giving it up, and we discussed the process and the need for self-kindness in the change process. The next day, I gave up chocolate. There have only been a few moments in the past weeks that I have thought I would love some chocolate, and when that happens, I use my mindfulness skills to notice, accept, and let go. Now that I don't have a daily habit of chocolate, I only eat some on special occasions with friends. I have three chocolate bars sitting at home and they will certainly be part of my handing-in-my-manuscript celebration. Until then, I am savoring mint tea! My intuition is right—I feel like I have more energy and focus without the chocolate. I am so glad I listened to it.

Slow Down to Think Up

Your brilliance or intuition comes from slowing down, checking in, and listening to your intuitive messages or inner wisdom. The voice within you is developed with the practice of calm. Each time you follow your intuition, you develop and strengthen that very important aspect of yourself and consequently, a sense of positivity.

Have you noticed we often get inspirations in the shower when the warm water is relaxing us and we have let go of the day and the strain? For many people, this is the most relaxing part of the day.

When we are relaxed, the brain goes into an alpha state and attention is more inward and focused on the senses. We get out of our heads and into our bodies. This allows for the brain to make associations, connecting new information to what is already on file, and for the brilliance of our intuition to emerge. Educators who know this will give their students brain breaks every 30 minutes. Short, energizing breaks can make all the difference when you are learning new material or have been focused on your work for a while.

Have you ever been in a situation where you cannot recall the name of a person or you lost your car keys? You are racking your brain to figure it out and nothing happens. As soon as you let go and redirect your attention, the name of the person appears or the location of the keys is revealed in a flash.

Carnegie Mellon neuroscientist David Creswell found in his research that people who distracted themselves from complex problem-solving tasks did better than those who put in conscious effort with no breaks. The surprising part is how fast the effect takes hold—only two minutes of distraction time was needed for their unconscious to kick in. Maybe that's why creative jobs often have basketball nets set up for the staff to just take a few shots to relax and step away from work.

Take a Brilliance Break

Make the time in your day to take a brilliance break. Take a walk in nature, work on your hobby, do some craft project, shoot some hoops, stretch, or if you need it, take a power nap. When you engage in a pleasurable activity, it gives your mind a break from solution-searching and allows the subconscious to come up with solutions on its own. Einstein was famous for both his walks and his power naps. Inspiration and intuition tend to happen when we are not thinking. When we are relaxed, open, and receptive, information comes to us. Letting go is required for letting creative insight arrive.

I recently read that the Walt Disney Company uses a consultant who teaches mindfulness skills as a means to access creativity in their design department. In the stillness and awareness that mindfulness brings, one easily finds clarity as well as the ability to make unexpected connections, take in new information, and arrive at new insights or intuition.

᳁

The next chapter introduces you to the nudges, the living assignments I have used with my students and clients. They are simple and easy to integrate into your current lifestyle. You can begin anywhere. Just begin.

DISCOVER|MAKE|DO
use positivity to design brilliance in your day

- **Discover** the answer to: *What excites me today?*

- **Make** a "happy at work" vision board. (See Chapter 5.)

- **Do:** Ask a question. Trust the answer. Take inspired action.

᳁ᕽ᳁

nudges

DESIGNING LIFESTYLE HABITS

You have picked up this book because you want more calm and ease in your busy life. The simple tools of design (discover, make, do) and these nudge activities (small, daily, happy) provide the tools and rituals to expand calm in your day. A small, daily practice with purpose and pleasure makes the day become meaningful. I want to help you close the gap between intention and behavior by giving you tools that make a difference.

Nudges are short living assignments that allow you to quickly and uniquely design your day to support your needs and lifestyle. You can make them your own by starting with activities that fit your current lifestyle, or you can give yourself a challenge to hone a new habit.

When I teach, I ask my students to perform what I call *living assignments* each week. These are small, daily, and happy activities to bring relaxation, mindfulness, and positivity to your day.

I want this experience to be fun and applicable to you, so you will be choosing your own nudges from this book. I designed it as a flexible program in which you pick the practices that have meaning for you. I will expose you to the assignments I share with my students that change the relationship to the anxiety and stress we all experience. Calm is the antidote to busy, only if we apply it. These nudges provide a busy person with an enjoyable and practical way to build the skills of joy, compassion, and brilliance.

The key to lasting energy is our ability to quiet the mind, listen to the wisdom of our intuition, and act with common sense and integrity. If you are looking for a new way to live your life that brings you both reward and renewal, these calming practices are for you.

When I teach, I share the essential lifestyle habits for creating a calm mind-body foundation. The foundation is creating a calm mind through mindfulness, diet, and sleep. In your practice of designing calm, you will find how slowing down helps becoming intentional. This focus of practicing calm in small, daily, and happy practices builds sustainable lifestyle habits that enhance wellness.

Lifestyle habits can make a big impact on our well-being and work. We don't want to give up the taste of our daily lattes, staying up late to finish e-mails, checking Facebook, or eliminating takeout, yet if we knew the benefits of a changed lifestyle, we would run, not walk, toward building this foundation of calm.

Please don't despair: The nudges I share support all behavior change. One of the nudges I give my students on the first day of class, besides the breathing-awareness practice, is drinking water. They find this one simple, easy practice can make a big different in their attention span, focus, and energy level.

Pick a Nudge and Practice for a Month

To start, focus on implementing one nudge each month. Some people might see this approach as slow, but doing one practice at a time is actually efficient and effective because it is sustainable. You can commit to one thing successfully rather than trying to do too much too fast. Start small, like breathing in stillness for one minute a day. It is a doable practice. Select the ones that have the most pull for you and tailor them to your needs. In one year, you will create 12 calm practices that serve your life.

Each nudge is an activity you can integrate into your busy life without feeling overwhelmed. I developed these exercises for my students and clients who have full schedules, and if they can do them, so can you. In fact, they report the practices are restorative. I designed them to be small, simple, and easy to fit in a busy schedule.

These nudges will ask you to have a beginner's mind in harnessing self-compassion, kindness, and the *skillpower* needed to create your best self. When we are calm, happy, and engaged, it makes it easier to follow healthy lifestyle practices like eating well, drinking water, doing movements you love, and getting a good night's sleep.

Use the Three R's

How you start the morning can create the flow of your day. Create a routine, ritual, or rave of pleasure that brings beauty and direction for your day. Let's explore how you can use the three R's of change: *routine*, *ritual*, and *rave*.

Our routines are how we move through each day without thinking. Designing some calm, positive practices in your daily routine can make it easier to shift toward the positive emotions of abiding calmness. Routines provide a sense of comfort. Once we establish a healthy routine, we no longer have to think about it.

Rituals are distinctive ways we go about the routines of our day. Rituals become anchors we have in our day to keep us grounded and present. You might think about what rituals you already have in your life. Many people give a prayer of thanks before eating. My parents have a ritual of turning on soothing music, saying grace, and appreciating the beauty of the meal before eating. This is an easy ritual of mindful eating that induces calm and pleasure, which supports nourishing ourselves.

A rave is about putting pleasure into the change process. It is important to make new practices happy for yourself. One way we can to this is to make them doable. Think about taking small steps.

Create a Daily Ritual

Creating rituals around your calm routine strengthens it. A morning ritual can bring forth the best in your day. Discover a simple practice that can make a big difference in how you move through the day and what you get accomplished. You can set a morning intention with a single word, quote, or passage of scripture to inspire the start of the day. For example, a word I love is *enthusiasm.* Lead your day with enthusiasm. Walk with enthusiasm. See what a difference it makes in your interactions.

Make a midday ritual of movement. This is a wonderful time to eat well, stretch, and connect with others. Lunch with others or a take a walk to a nearby plaza or park and enjoy the feeling of community. Taking a midday break can refresh and energize you to use the afternoon effectively. Give your mind and body a break and stretch. Get out of the building and get some fresh air.

Walk around the block. Clearing the body of stuck energy also clears the mind and allows for new thinking.

Rituals are important at home and work. Many of us have rituals at work that can either help us or hinder us. When you get to work, have you noticed as soon as you open e-mails, you get sidetracked from your original idea? Perhaps you can hold off on the e-mail and start work with your most important project for the first few hours. Save your urgent e-mails for after you have completed two hours of your own work. If you take this advice, make sure to let your clients, friends, and family know not to e-mail you but to call you with concerns that need immediate attention.

Keep a Design Notebook

As mentioned, keeping a notebook is one of the main tools of a designer. As you are building your skills of a designer's mind (*discover, make, do*), writing and drawing are keys to your progress and creativity. Writing and drawing help anchor your goals for the day and your dreams for a lifetime. I have kept some kind of notebook since my teens. I have written diaries, travel journals, gratitude journals, art and yoga notebooks, and business-design notebooks.

Here are a few ideas on how to squeeze writing into a busy schedule from my friend Lesley Foster, who teaches journaling in Charlottesville. You can write quite a bit in a short amount of time, especially if you keep your pen moving and don't edit your writing. Think about "capturing your thoughts instead of composing." Keep your pen on the paper and write through the pauses using phrases like, "What else? What else?" See what emerges in a ten-minute writing session. I keep a small notebook in my bag and use the Notes app on my iPhone, but you can also use notecards, paper napkins, or any slip of paper, like a receipt.

- Write in the parking lot.
- Write in little pockets of time, like lunch breaks or while waiting for meetings to start.
- Write lists.
- Doodle or scribble images.

Make It Pleasurable

Lastly, *rave* refers to making these routines and rituals pleasurable. Simple pleasures can bring inspiration and energy to your intention to bring the best to your day. Design some simple happiness in your day. Drinking your morning tea or coffee from a favorite mug while reviewing the plans for the day is a relaxing morning ritual that brings pleasure.

One example of a rave that a student shared with me was meeting a friend for lunch on Fridays at Feast, a favorite local food store in Charlottesville. This ritual of sharing a leisurely meal with a friend was one of the highlights in her busy school schedule. Taking time to slow down and savor is a practice that invites more intimate connection and conversation.

How can you make the routines of your day have rituals and raves?

Use your notebook and do a three-minute writing on this question. Then review and make a list of ways to make each day have pleasure. Create your own ritual from your list.

End the Day with Gratitude

Ending the day is just as important as beginning the day. To me, the most important part of the day is when I am asleep. One of my favorite evening rituals is to wind down my thinking by looking at home design magazines. I spend some time just paging through a magazine looking at the beautiful pictures of homes and imaging how I want my new home. I find looking at beauty a relaxing and pleasurable activity to soothe my mind to slumber. When I have a good night's sleep, my day goes well.

Many people I speak to are concerned about sleep. Some self-proclaimed busy people are under some misperception that sleep is optional. Sleep helps with the function of all the body's systems, including memory and learning.

One nudge I have honed in my life is getting a good night's sleep. Years ago, I had difficulty sleeping. I dug into the sleep research and discovered some simple ways to create an environment and routine that allows me eight to ten hours of a solid good night's sleep. When we are well rested, our day is more relaxed, and we are more attentive to the moment. With a good night's sleep, we have a greater capacity to respond effectively to those habits that seem difficult to change.

I remember attending a conference and hearing some of the neuroscience research on the brain and meditation. I sat in on a great dialogue between the Dalai Lama and a group of scientists. They all agreed a consistent good night's sleep was more important than meditation. Start with the basics and build from there. Sleep helps create memory and good recall.

Did you know a good night's sleep relates to the amount of water and the quality of food we eat? Have you ever had a Coke and chocolate bar and tried to fall asleep? How about a turkey sandwich? Certain foods at the end of the day can induce us into slumber. Again the mind-body connection is demonstrated here with these simple examples.

Find the foods that soothe you to slumber and use them in the evening. Keep the high-intensity foods like caffeine and tea to the morning or midday. Eat lightly in the evening so sleep comes easily. Have your bigger meals in the earlier part of the day for energy and stamina. When you have energy, you get more done in less time because you can concentrate and relax. Here are some tips I learned to help get a good night's sleep: take a hot shower, sauna, or lavender and Epsom salt bath an hour before bed; sleep in a dark and cool room (a cooler core body temperature means better sleep); have real plants in your room; sleep in organic and natural fiber sheets and pj's; and get a good pillow or two.

Make a plan to slumber longer. What you need is eight to nine hours of sleep at night. Create a routine, ritual, and rave to wind down before sleep. Do my nudge called the "grateful heart" body scan before sleep. It will help you relax and fall asleep with mental images and a feeling of gratitude. When we practice gratitude we are practicing mindfulness. As we end the day with thoughts of gratitude each night, we naturally become more aware and awake to gratitude during the day.

There is a reason it's called "beauty sleep": Your body needs the renewal. I want you to make your day beautiful, and sleep is a prerequisite. A good night's sleep will definitely support the rave factor.

One Good Day: An Example

Here is what one good day might look like using nudges. As I said before, make sure to make it yours. There are many ways to design a day. Here is one way to include a variety of simple rituals that can make a powerful difference.

Morning

- Wake up: stretch, smile, and breathe.

- Drink a glass of water with lemon.

- Look with wonder at your face in the mirror.

- Morning reflection: Write in your notebook an intention and attitude for the day.

- Sit in stillness for one minute.

- Eat a real, whole-food breakfast, mindfully and with gratitude.

- Savor a cup of tea.

- Walk or drive cheerfully to work or school.

- Smile and breathe while working.

- Take brain breaks of stretching, breathing, and laughing.

- Drink water.

Afternoon

- Eat a real-food lunch with gratitude. Get outside into nature if possible.

- Stretch, breathe, and smile while at work.

- Drink water.

- Savor a treat such as mint tea and chocolate.

- Walk or drive home with gratitude; play fun music.

Evening

- Arrive home and drink water with a dash of lime.

- Shake off the day with some movement, breathing, or talking to a friend.

- Appreciate and savor a real-food dinner.

- Visit with family and friends, see a movie, laugh, play in the garden, or do yoga.

- Evening reflection: Write in your gratitude notebook and read a prayer or poem.

- Give thanks.

- Go to bed early; relax and fall asleep with a feeling of gratitude.

The Nudges

Now that I've discussed how to use the nudges, let's get into the nudges themselves!

Hammocking

I highly recommend getting a hammock and spending some time just being. *Hammocking* is now a verb on university campuses. Students are using portable hammocks to find some time alone and to relax. I want you to do the same: Take some time each day to let your mind and body relax. Practice daydreaming. The quality of your life does depend on what you do. Daydreaming allows your mind to wander, create, and imagine the possibilities. When not directed, the mind tends to unravel into anxiety and fear. It finds worry. So direct your mind in the direction of your dreams and revel in relaxation. Relaxation helps in stabilizing attention.

As your mind and body relax, a quality of calm presence can be cultivated. Acceptance is a form of self-care and self-kindness. By simply paying attention to ourselves in stillness, the body and mind naturally slow down and unravel tension and mental strain. When we are in a state of calmness, we can move forward freely and effectively. Saying yes to now is powerful. The hammock is the perfect place to cultivate these qualities.

So how do we let go and relax?

Start by realizing that holding stress harms you and that you have a choice. It's not personal; it's physiological. We are wired to be alert and reactive. By taking short and frequent calming breaks, you can dissipate the built-up tension of the day and create a new pattern and way of being.

One of the exercises I do at work to release stress is to take regular stretching breaks. When I worked at the University of Virginia, I kept my printer down the hall in the office manager's room so that I had to get up and stretch. As I walked down the hall, I did all kinds of stretching. In addition, I got current updates from my co-worker that enhanced our communication and collaboration.

While there are many places to stretch out and relax, I like the hammock. Let your hammock practice guide you to the quiet magnificence within you. The place of possibilities happens when you are calm, accepting, positive, and resonating with what is meaningful and beautiful to you. Savor the beauty of the moment and allow ideas to flow. Time in the hammock allows for insights and allows you to rest in the images of your resolution.

This method of relaxing is a wonderful contemplative step toward your future. The relaxing hammock practice of stillness is perfect, as it nestles you in nature surrounded by beauty and connects you to that quiet source of inner wisdom. Relaxation puts you in a receptive mode. *Voilà!* Inspiration arrives. You can't seek inspiration. You have to set up the condition for its arrival. The gifts you get from relaxation are many. I want you to have them all. Set a time for daily relaxation. Remember to start by keeping your relaxation practice small, daily, and happy.

Nudge: five-minute weekly hammock relaxation practice

- Find a place of quiet and silence in your hammock (or bed).

- Lie down and get comfortable.

- Start with yawn breathing. (See yawn breathing nudge.)

- Open your jaw and make some fake yawns.

- Allow the mind to wander and relax.

- Let your eyes close and soften.

- Relax and do some soft belly breathing.

- Notice the rise and fall of the belly as you relax.

- Let go of any tension in the body and worries in the mind.

- Shift your focus onto your senses, feeling your body breathe.

- Shift or stretch your body.
- Shift from thinking to feeling or sensing.
- Connect with the beauty of your breath.
- Watch the wave of the breath.
- Allow gravity to hold you as you relax deeply.

Belly Breathing

The cornerstone to managing our energy is learning to relax. Finding joyful ways to relax the body and calm the mind deepens our capacity for being with the beauty of our body's wisdom and natural intelligence. Peacefulness is an inner stillness that starts with relaxation. Breathing practices are the mind-body guide to relaxation. Allowing the body and mind to relax, the mind's power—the ability to direct attention—is harnessed.

The breath is a tool we use to both relax and hone our attention. It's so interesting how taking some deep, full breaths can be both relaxing and energizing at the same time. Most of us have gotten into the habit of shallow breathing as a result of our rushed pace. This is merely a habit that can be changed and shaped with practice.

My students love the various breathing practices I introduce to them over the semester. The belly breathing practice is by far the most popular. They often tell me stories of going back to their dorm and encountering a stressed-out roommate. Because belly breathing is so simple, they become the teachers and share the lesson of this practice with their roommates. I love that they find this activity to be so valuable for themselves that they feel compelled to share it with others. If we all had access to some of these simple tools, we would improve our health and well-being.

Learning this basic breathing skill will bring enhanced results for relaxing the body and developing a quiet mind. We can't think our way to calm. We need to breathe and feel our way to calm.

Deep belly breathing is something you can do anywhere. Imagine a baby sleeping in a crib and how their belly goes up and down. This is the image and feeling you want to experience: the rise and fall of the breath in your body. Following the breath as it moves through the body is a simple yet powerful practice. Every out breath is an opportunity to let go and relax.

Many of us are breathing upside down. My grandmother used to tell me to stick my stomach in and stand up straight. This posture results in what most of us are doing: chest breathing. Taking small, shallow breaths from the upper chest. There is nothing wrong with that other than that it is a breath of fear. If your body gets messages that you are afraid, then it sends all kinds of messages to protect itself. These messages produce the stress hormones, like cortisol, that make it difficult to get to sleep or to lose weight.

Harvard cardiologist Herbert Benson is my guru when it comes to relaxation. He is a pioneer in mind-body medicine and researches the importance that the relaxation practice has for health and well-being. He has discussed the value of relaxation with the Dalai Lama and other scientists as part of the Mind and Life talks. It's difficult to be mindful and compassionate when we are not relaxed. Learning relaxation is the first step of mindfulness. Quieting the mind is valuable for the brain; it allows time for the brain to process information gained in the day.

Belly breathing is the first step to begin to relax the mind and body. The immediate benefits of this breathing are that it quiets the mind, reduces cravings, and relaxes the body by balancing the nervous system. The long-range benefits are greater emotional control, increased perceptual sensitivity, and increased mental clarity. Practice this exercise throughout your day for feeling your best.

Nudge: one minute of belly breathing

- Sit quietly and comfortably in a chair, settle in, and feel your pelvic bones.

- Lengthen your spine. Lift, release, and relax your shoulders.

- Feel your feet flat on the floor.

- Place your hands on your belly.

- Follow the rise and fall of the breath.

- Let the belly rise on the in breath.

- Let the belly fall on the out breath.

- Allow the sides of your rib cage to expand and contract just like an accordion.

- Let go of any tension on the out breath.

- Remember that every out breath is an opportunity to let go and relax.

- Enjoy the feeling of calm energy.

Aware Breathing

Aware breathing builds on belly breathing and is so easy. We manage our energy through awareness. Having a breath-awareness practice hones the ability to reduce stress and annoying fear-based thinking. When we are centered during awareness, we are open and receptive. Calm allows us to take on new possibilities. When we realize we create peace in the same way we create worry, we have freedom and access our ability to choose.

Aware breathing, or nasal breathing, is a powerful breath that calms and centers our energy and builds the quality of mindfulness. As we use this self-care practice, we can easily shift from a thinking mode to a sensing mode, allowing for greater clarity. We begin to connect the qualities of calmness with this simple breath. I like the ease of aware breath and its availability. You can do this breathing virtually anywhere. It can be particularly helpful if you get anxious or frustrated while waiting in lines or traffic. It has a natural calming effect, yet it energizes. Simply bringing awareness to your breathing can begin to shift the frustrating thoughts that can occur in a difficult situation.

I have given this tool to my students to use at work and school. I recently ran into one of my former MBA students who was so excited to see me because he said, "This is the one breathing practice that I use before my business negotiation meetings." He explained his business meetings were challenging and he needs to stand his ground. The aware breathing gave him a simple practice he can use a few minutes before negotiations to create the calm focus needed to listen and respond effectively.

We need these tools of transformation in the high-stressed world we live in today. Often we can't change our work, but we can change how we approach our work, beginning with calmness and clarity. This tool is one I recommend to everyone because it can be used in so many situations. The fun begins when you witness some of life's challenges turn into creative situations.

It was psychologist Jon Kabat-Zinn who inspired me to cultivate the qualities of mindfulness. Kabat-Zinn is the founding executive director for the Center for Mindfulness in Medicine at the University of Massachusetts. His teaching and research made mindfulness popular and part of a healthy wellness lifestyle. I took his mindfulness-based stress-reduction course many years ago and learned the value of breathing not only as a tool for relaxation but also as a focal point for bringing me calmly into the present moment.

The benefits of an awareness-breathing practice are that it brings you into the present moment and relaxes you. Awareness breathing is helpful in conversations to increase your ability to be a deep listener, remain calm in heated situations, and enhance clarity and decision making.

Nudge: one minute of aware breathing

- Begin by bringing attention to the feeling of breath.

- Feel the breath as it flows in and out of the nostrils.

- Notice there is a slight touch of coolness on the inhalation.

- Notice a slight touch of warmth on the exhalation.

- Allow your breathing to be even and relaxed.

- Stay with an even breath.

- As your mind wanders, gently bring it back to the awareness of breathing.

- Breathe comfortably in and out through the nostrils.

- Throughout the practice of breathing, become aware of sensations in your body.

- Stay with these observations with kindness and curiosity.

- Notice your thoughts wander in, and come back to your breath.

- Enjoy the sensation of breathing with awareness.

Yawn Breathing

We know that stretching helps reduce stress and tension in the body that builds up throughout the day. It is a good thing to take the time to stretch and move. But did you know that when you yawn you are stretching the jaw, which holds much of your daily tension? When we are stressed, our bodies tighten up and a daily stretching routine can keep stress from accumulating. Incorporating a stretch break in your daily routine is a practice of building balance and resiliency. This is especially true if you have a desk job. Our bodies were meant to move. Stretching keeps the muscles supple and strong. I encourage you to use some of your favorite stretches to get the kinks out of your body. Do this a few times a day, especially if you work at a computer. When we are stressed or overly focused on our computers, we hold tension in our body and particularly in the jaw.

Yawn breathing helps us stretch and release the muscles around the jaw, face, and neck. The nice thing about yawn breathing is that it is a practice you can do at your desk or as you walk down the hall to the copy machine. It probably should not be done during an important business meeting. My students love this practice because yawning is contagious. As soon as we begin, the whole class is sighing with relaxation. They leave the class refreshed, energized, and ready to take on the next part of their day.

I first learned about this practice in the book *How God Changes Your Brain* by Dr. Andrew Newberg and Mark Waldman. It is listed as the fifth best way to exercise your brain. Yawning has been used for decades in voice therapy and in acting classes as an effective tool to reduce performance anxiety. Their research found yawning is not only relaxing, but also brings you into a heightened state of cognitive awareness.

The benefits of yawn breathing include released muscle tension, increased oxygen, and supplying the body with more energy. Conscious yawning generates a deep sense of relaxation, calmness, and alertness.

Nudge: one minute of yawn breathing

- Begin by taking some slow, deep breaths.

- Relax the jaw by stretching your mouth open.

- Do this a few times, and then make a long, sighing sound.

- Make the action of yawning. After about four or five fake yawns, some real yawns will come.

- Notice what happens in your mouth, throat, chest, and belly.

- Release the tension in the jaw. Relax and loosen all the facial muscles.

- Allow for more oxygen as you breathe.

- Repeat for ten yawns. Pause in between for a few seconds.

- Allow yourself to stretch your arms and shoulders as you continue yawning.

- Now just relax into your natural breath.

Smile Breathing

Everyone is beautiful with a smile. One way to get grounded is to just smile and breathe. It is simple self-care. The mind-body connection is powerful, and a smile floods the body with chemicals and hormones of happiness as you crinkle your eyes and curl the corners of your lips upward.

Often we can't change our mood with just thinking; we need to shift our body as well. Smiling is an easy way to do so. Think of it as a mini yoga pose; as you smile repeatedly, your mood changes. Smiling strengthens the brain's neural ability to maintain a positive outlook. This type of wholesome beauty is a natural, effortless state as we move through the day with a smile of appreciation.

Smiling is a small facial movement that can make a big impact on your day. When you shift your body, your mind will follow. After a minute of smiling, you will be conjuring up positive thoughts, memories, and ideas.

I want to introduce you to the practice of smile breathing as a way to increase positivity in your day. It is a self-kindness practice to use throughout the day. We have all heard the accolades of positive thinking. We cannot always change our thoughts. When we shift our body, like going for a walk or even talking to a friend, our energy and feelings naturally shift.

Smile breathing is a simple shifting of the body with a smile and breath focus. You can begin by allowing a smile to enter the mind creating an inner smile. Then allow the smile muscles to brighten as you continue to breathe. A small but powerful shift like this can be used anytime and anywhere. Smile breathing is a living assignment I give my students as a way to introduce pleasure and reduce stress in their day-to-day life. Smile breathing while walking to class, studying at the library, or waiting for class to begin can make an impact on how you interact with the task at hand.

I first learned about smile breathing from studying the work of Thich Nhat Hanh, a popular Vietnamese Buddhist monk who teaches mindfulness. Since then, I have reviewed research that indicates smiling stimulates brain circuits that enhance social interaction, empathy, and mood. I remember a headline in a magazine that has stayed with me over the years, "Smile Beauty Inspires."

Nudge: one minute of smile breathing

- For one minute, focus on gentle breathing.

- Begin with observing where you feel the breath in the body.

- As you inhale allow a smile to enter the mind—an inner smile.

- Invite the smile muscles to brighten as you continue to breathe slowly.

- You may find memories of generosity, laughter, and gratefulness follow the breath.

- Drop the thoughts and stay with the feeling of smiling.

- Allow the feelings of the smile to cascade throughout your body.

- Finally, bring a smile to your face and continue feeling and observing.

- The jaw naturally relaxes as you smile.

- Breathe in calm, breathe out a smile.

- Begin to notice the body and senses as you relax and smile.

- Take this smile into the rest of your day.

The Undo

The undo is an important component of a mindfulness practice. Mindfulness starts with bringing awareness to the body. The undo is a body-scan practice that grounds us in the present moment and releases stress. It not only hones awareness but also makes a shift in how you hold and let go of stress stored in the body. This practice is usually done at the end of every yoga class to integrate the energy of the yoga movements. It is a stillness practice of letting the body unwind and relax fully. It focuses on your ability to trust and let earth's gravity hold you as you release muscle strain.

We all need the undo. As we move through our day, we pick up all kinds of emotional and physical stressors, and we can use this practice of renewal to calm the body and mind. You will find that in the grounding body scan, you build the capacity to listen to your body so you can fully attend to it. The intention of this practice is not to feel any different, to relax, or to be calm. These things may happen or they may not. Instead, the intention of the practice is, as best you can, to bring awareness to any sensations you detect as you focus your attention on each part of the body. This in turn grounds you in the present moment.

Read the steps of this grounding body scan to familiarize yourself with the process. Then, see if you can let go of the instructions and just follow the steps in your mind. In my class, we roll out the yoga mats, do some light stretching, and then lie down to begin the relaxing body scan. This 15- to 20-minute practice has a profound effect on my students. They often report feeling refreshed and energized as we roll up the mats to start the next part of the class. My students love this practice to unwind at the end of the day, and they often share it with their friends. This is particularly good to use as a method to fall asleep or a process to get your 20-minute cat nap off to a good start.

The undo *is* doing something. It is releasing the tensions of the day. The body scan has been studied by many researchers in the field of mindfulness as an important practice for tuning in to the body's awareness. The body scan is one of the key elements of *yoga nidra* that has been studied to reduce the harmful effects of trauma. Yoga teacher and researcher Dr. Richard Miller has shown that the yoga nidra, the deep body-awareness practice, reduces chronic pain and depression in soldiers who are experiencing post-traumatic stress disorder.

The benefits of the undoing with a body scan are greater awareness of the body, release of strain in the muscles, letting the mind empty, and feeling energy in the body.

Nudge: do the undo

The following are the steps of a body scan, which is a practice you can do before sleeping. It will support you in feeling centered, grounded, aware, and present.

- Lie down and allow your body to let go and relax.

- Allow your eyes to close gently.

- Take a few moments to feel your breath and the sensations of breathing.

- Feel the physical sensations in your body as you breathe.

- On each out breath allow your body to let go, sink a little deeper into bed.

- Let gravity hold you as you settle into your body awareness.

- Bring your awareness to the physical sensations in your lower abdomen.

- Be aware of the rise and fall of the breath.

- Next bring the focus of your awareness to the legs.

- Focus on the toes and feet to investigate the quality of the sensations.

- Notice the sense of contact between your toes, a sense of tingling, or warmth.

- Let your awareness move to your legs and allow them to relax.

- Create a wave of breath in your body.

- As the breath lets go on the out breath, let go of your legs completely.

- Allow your awareness to move into relaxing all parts of your body—the calf, shin, knee, and thighs.

- Continue to bring awareness to your physical sensations in each part of your body—the pelvic area, back, chest, fingers, hands, arms, shoulders, neck, head, and face. In each area bring gentle curiosity to bodily sensations that are present.

- As you leave each major area, breathe and let go of that region on the out breath.

- Become aware of tension or other intense sensations in a particular part of your body. Breathe into them using the in breath to bring gentle awareness right into the sensations.

- As best you can have a sense of letting go—or releasing—on the out breath.

- The mind will inevitably wander away from the breath and the body from time to time. That is entirely normal. When you notice it, gently acknowledge it and return your attention to the part of the body you intended to focus on.

- After you have scanned the whole body, sense the body as a whole.

- Breathe flowing freely in and out of the body.

BEEM–Body, Emotion, Environment, and Mind

Mindful-awareness training cultivates the capacity for us to be present in the moment. Mindfulness requires that we slow down and spend some time in stillness and silence. Similar to the undo practice of the body scan, this practice develops our qualities of awareness, acceptance, and compassion.

BEEM is awareness of the qualities of the Body, Emotion, Environment, and Mind. This is a helpful practice to take in the fullness of the moment by shifting your attention to sounds, senses, thoughts, and feelings.

Being aware and accepting of the present-moment experience is so satisfying. Our lives need acceptance and attention. This practice hones your ability to cultivate awareness of all of the landscapes within and around you. As you pay attention, notice, and observe, you begin to sense a spaciousness that opens you up to possibilities beyond your thinking mind.

This awareness practice allows you to be aware, observe, and accept with self-kindness. As we look at habits with the eyes of self-kindness, the reactive patterns naturally unravel. There is nothing to do: The doing happens in the process of awareness. I encourage my students to pay attention in a way that is gentle and kind. Dan Harris, TV anchor and author of the book

10% Happier, recently stated at the Wisdom 2.0 Business conference: "Mindfulness is having awareness of your thoughts and being okay with it." Learning mindfulness is a profound exercise in my classroom. It heightens my students' ability to pay attention to the coming and going of sound, feelings, thoughts, and emotions. They discover that at each moment there is newness. They don't have to believe everything they think.

The present moment is a place of choice. Presence is power. Accept everything. Be present with whatever happens to want your attention. Be discerning. We don't have to do anything about it. We can simply notice, breathe, drift, notice again, and repeat. Pay attention without giving in to your judgments. This practice is about noticing with kind eyes. We will not like everything we see. Each moment is not glorious. Life is rich with ups and downs. There is something wonderfully liberating about saying yes to the messy feelings in life. Acceptance without grasping is the key to mindful attention.

When you center yourself in mindful awareness, you let in a calmer, neutral alignment where discernment can be used in making decisions. Shifting into a neutral space allows you to see the opportunities that may seem to be surrounded by adversity. By staying neutral, you lighten the stress load and keep yourself open to possibilities. It is the middle path that is steady and strong.

Nudge: five minutes of BEEM— Body, Emotion, Environment, and Mind

- Begin with body awareness. Sit with your eyes closed, bring your attention to your body, and simply observe.

- Scan and notice where there is strain or comfort. Focus on your physical body.

- Watch your breath rise and fall.

- Notice your posture and the color or lack of color behind your eyelids.

- Bring your attention to your feet, toes, heels, and balls of the feet.

- Scan your whole body, noticing sensations like muscle tension, taste, hunger, fullness, temperature, pain, or discomfort. Take a few breaths.

- Shift your attention to your emotions. What feelings do you notice?

- Simply notice the flow of feeling and the energy of your emotions. Notice how feelings are located in different areas of your body and how they change as you shift the body or thinking. Take a few breaths.

- Shift your attention to the environment, everything outside of you: smells in the air, the texture of fabric on your skin. Open up to sounds and silence and the comings and goings of sensations that relate to air or breeze. Notice the space and pleasure or comfort associated with them. Notice and then take a few breaths.

- Shift your attention to your thoughts. Notice the coming and going of thoughts, just like the coming and going of sounds, emotions, and so on. Simply notice the changing mental landscape. Notice your state of mind, stories, themes, pictures, and memories arriving and leaving.

- Take a few breaths, then come back to your body awareness and notice your breath.

Loving-Kindness

Loving-kindness starts with directing kindness to yourself. One way to begin to view your life with kindness is by shifting your thinking from critical to curious. We are so hard on ourselves. Knowing that the mind has an inner critic, the voice of judgment, is the first step to realizing that we don't have to take that voice seriously. This realization can help us soften that voice and invite curiosity instead.

When the voice comes up that says, "I'm not good enough," "He doesn't love me," or "I'm not smart enough," just notice it with some gentle curiosity. See if other questions arise. Instead, ask yourself: "What if I am good enough?" "What if he does love me?" "What if I am smart enough?" This form of self-compassion can arise naturally in many life circumstances, and it is also something that you can cultivate. A loving-kindness practice supports you in being gentle with difficult feelings and challenges in life. That certainly has been true for me.

One year, I bought myself a dozen roses every few weeks as an act of self-kindness. When the flowers were ready to be tossed, I would pull off the old petals and scatter them on my walkway. For this particular year, having roses was a way for me to be kind and loving to myself. There are so many ways you can introduce kindness to your day. As you allow yourself to feel your own love and well-being, a loving-kindness practice can help you expand your awareness so you can experience self-kindness in more ways throughout your day.

The research on a loving-kindness practice shows that over time this type of practice changes the way people approach life. Positive psychologist Barbara Fredrickson, who wrote the book *Positivity*, has spent years studying the practice of loving-kindness as a tool for happiness and connection. She concludes that a nine-week practice of loving-kindness can lead to shifts in people's daily experiences of a wide range of positive emotions, including love, joy, gratitude, contentment, hope, pride, interest, amusement, and awe. Her book *Love 2.0* explains that love is the greatest source of sustainable happiness and well-being.

The loving-kindness practice below is part of mindfulness training. It focuses on the quality of self-compassion and then extends it to others. A loving-kindness practice can be powerful as it calms the mind and keeps you connected to your heart.

Nudge: start your morning with a one-minute loving-kindness practice

- Sit comfortably, breathe, and relax. Bring your hand to your heart.

- Bring to mind a difficult situation or some stress in your present life.

- Send a message of love, care, and acceptance to whatever feeling is arising.

- Say to yourself, *Even though I have this feeling, I completely love and accept myself.*

- Repeat the following loving-kindness blessing in your mind: *May I be filled with love. May I be well. May I be peaceful and at ease. May I be happy.* (You can adjust the words in any way that feels comfortable to you.)

- Repeat these phrases again and again for a full minute. Let any feelings arise with these words. Let the feelings permeate your body and your mind.

- Allow yourself to have self-kindness and compassion for your feelings.

Savoring Calm

Savoring calm and happy memories is a quick way to boost relaxation and positivity. Most of us have a memory of a pleasant and relaxing time in our lives. It could be a relaxing day on a warm beach, time in a hammock, or a night alone near a cozy fire reading a good book. When we recall positive memories, our body responds as if it were happening in the moment, and we begin to feel a flood of all the good feelings from this time in our life. Our imagination can make some real changes in the body, and savoring happy times of calm can be just the break we need.

What are some of your most relaxing activities? One of my favorite relaxation practices is taking a hot soak. At the end of a long day, I love taking a good long bath in a tub filled with Epsom salts and lavender. These salts contain magnesium, a mineral that relaxes the muscles, and the lavender is soothing. This is an excellent way to undo the day. All the stress and strain just runs down the drain. Just remembering this relaxing activity now is beginning to soothe me—and it also reminds me to schedule this into my day!

Another way to savor is to review the many moments of happiness I experienced in the day. By recalling the best parts of the day, I naturally move my focus to gratitude and appreciation. I might do this while I am taking my warm bath, when I sit down to write in my design notebook, or when I am falling asleep in the evening. This steady form of remembering happiness daily calms the body and creates a habit of happy awareness. Just feeling the warmth and sensation of recalling these memories begins to conjure up joy.

Yesterday, I had a particularly wonderful evening with my family. We took a hike and then grilled using the fresh food we got from the Saturday farmers' market. Throughout the next day, as I worked, I savored the feeling of well-being. Fred Bryant, the co-author of the book *Savoring: A New Model of Positive Experience* and a social psychologist at Loyola University Chicago, describes savoring as "swishing [the experience] around in one's mind." Savoring our best experiences in our minds maximizes our capacity for joy.

Savoring calm and pleasant memories is a way to continue to keep these qualities alive in your life and expand the joy factor. The benefits of savoring include stronger relationships, improved mental and physical health, and finding more creative solutions to problems.

Nudge: spend the day savoring calm and happiness

Consider incorporating some or all of these suggestions in your day, and feel free to come up with some of your own.

- Share your good feelings with others.

- Remember moments of a loved one's smile, chuckle, or touch.

- Explore all the senses with mindful attention: the beauty, sounds, smells, taste, or touch.

- Congratulate yourself and revel in your small successes.

- Appreciate loved ones. Say "I love you" and "thank you" out loud.

- Outwardly express your good feelings. Laugh out loud, and jump or shout for joy.

- Leave love notes.

- Allow your breath to be even and relaxed as you savor and enjoy the feelings.

Listen Deeply

When you are listening to people speak, do you find yourself thinking about other things? In the middle of a conversation, do you realize you have not heard a word of what the other person has said? This happens to all of us. What can we do to stay present with the person speaking?

I ask my first-year students, "Who doesn't listen to you?" They say, "My parents." Helping my students become good listeners can often change their conversations with their parents. Giving the spaciousness of allowing another to talk without interrupting can be powerful. The greatest barrier to effective listening is to make immediate judgments, to assume, guess, or get defensive. When we have a viewpoint of openness, it makes it easier to listen fully, remain calm, and hear what the other has to say.

I was recently speaking to a group of breast-cancer survivors in Richmond, Virginia, and afterward a woman came up to me to tell me her son had taken my Mindful Leadership class when he was a first-year student at the University of Virginia. He had graduated and had since been out in the working world for the past few years. She clearly remembered he took my class because he changed his behavior after the class on mindful listening. Before, when he called his mom, it was all about him. After the class on mindful listening, he asked his mother about her day. He used the skills we practiced in class and listened thoughtfully, often following up with clarifications and deepening questions. This had a big impact on their relationship. She said it changed his life. I think it changed hers. We cannot underestimate the impact of our actions on other people.

It is amazing when you take the time to slow down and have meaningful, rich, and quality conversations. This time of slowing down is going to expand your productivity. When our communications are clear, our connections deepen, allowing for greater compassion and love.

Mindful listening has been studied as a way to enhance communication in the professional world by making communication more transparent and effective. It is a very rich practice in building relationships. This form of effective listening can strengthen and provide a quality of communication that enhances intimacy, creates partnerships, and produces collaborations and creativity.

Nudge: deep listening

Here are a few ways to get started with deep listening. Try the following the next time you are with family or friends.

- Bring your full attention and make eye contact. Even on the phone, imagine the eye contact.

- Concentrate on what the others are saying.
- Listen fully by taking in the words and feelings that are being conveyed.
- Notice your urge to interrupt.
- Continue to listen and breathe.
- Relax into the action of listening.
- Listen and observe for feelings.
- Stay with your breathing as you continue to listen.
- Listen to learn or comprehend, to discern, to support, and to appreciate.

Savor a Beautiful Day

A beautiful day is about creating and integrating small, intentional thoughts and behaviors into your day to make it meaningful. Using this power of intention can create more beauty, self-kindness, and compassion in your daily routine. Extend this essence of compassion to others by designing a beautiful day for yourself. As you enjoy the day, others will be curious.

My students love this exercise, which was first introduced by Martin Seligman, one of the founders of positive psychology. Of course you'd be pleased if your day meets or goes beyond your expectation. The trick is that if things don't go your way, you can still find the beauty. If you are following the savoring advice, you will find something beautiful about the day. This practice of savoring a beautiful day builds the capacity to experience greater positive emotions like hope, connection, love, and joy.

When we have an intention for a beautiful day, the brilliance of life flows toward us. Planning to create an intention and actions of making your day beautiful makes living your best life possible. It creates meaning in your day-to-day routine. I can guarantee it won't be perfect, but with the right attitude it will be beautiful.

Creating happiness through meaningful gestures of kindness and compassion is a simple way to build a habit of well-being and happiness that is long-lasting. What if your only daily intention and action was to greet everyone you know with a smile and some twinkling eye contact? Just this simple behavior would make a lasting difference on your health and well-being as well as have a positive effect on others near you.

So how do we start saying yes to a meaningful and beautiful life?

Begin with the understanding that our lives don't need changing; they need acceptance. With acceptance, they may organically shift and change. When we move into acceptance, we are free, relaxed, and open.

Here is where we can insert a new habit, intention, and action that will build our resiliency with the day-to-day challenges.

Haven't we all had the thought, *If only I had a new house, or car, or job, my life would be different*? Our lives can become routine. Perhaps we do need to get going and make significant changes. It is the little changes that will help make the bigger changes happen at the right time and place. (This nudge is adapted from Martin Seligman's beautiful day activity.)

Nudge: design a beautiful day

- Pick a date in the next week and set aside time to design a beautiful day.

- Go through your day with the intention of experiencing its beauty. This could include time alone, time with friends, special meals, or walks in nature.

- Live the day fully appreciating the unexpected.

- Practice the techniques of savoring. Savor the day with others, including them in your plan. At the end of the day, savor the memories. Practicing the technique of savoring intensifies and lengthens positive emotions.

- Reflect on the following questions in your notebook:
  *What were the qualities of my beautiful day? Is there
  any other action I would take to move toward achiev-
  ing a "beautiful day" more regularly? How can I take
  the concept of a beautiful day into my life?*

Joy Walking

Moving the body can shift the mind. Einstein's daily
stroll cleared his mind and developed his senses as he
enjoyed savoring the time to amble. Let yourself see the
world. Colors, shapes, and sounds of the landscape can
all be points of reflection for our enjoyment. Walk with
awareness of nature, people, and place. Gaze upward. Joy
walking is restorative and calming. Movement creates a
connection to breathing, allowing for more oxygen. It
clears the mind. Remember, more oxygen means more
energy. Joy walking is about looking for the positive and
embracing the energy of life.

My yoga teacher poignantly said in class one day that
the opposite of depression is vitality. Walk to your daily
destination with a smile. Put on your favorite comfortable shoes and amble through your neighborhood. Practice leaving the iPod and cell phone at home. Walk with
awareness of your surroundings and take in the beauty
of nature and architecture. Be in the now. Tune in to all

your senses. This is a simple practice you can use anytime to hone your awareness to the senses. Listen to the sounds of nature mixed with the sounds of the street. Nature is healing and restorative. It connects you to appreciating natural beauty.

Peter Lambrou, one of the authors of *Code to Joy,* talks about unlocking the natural state of happiness and why nature can be calming. Nature is made up of fractals, repeating patterns that are identical or similar. Examples of fractals in nature are leaves, flowers, ocean waves, and snowflakes. Research has been done on the effect of fractal patterns on human psychology. It appears that we are hard-wired to respond to certain fractals in nature. This exposure in nature can reduce stress levels by as much as 60 percent.

Joy walking is a wonderful practice that incorporates everything we have practiced: breathing, awareness, and now the joy and gratitude of our environment. I like to joy walk in the morning to set my day. It is also great to use as I walk from building to building at work. My students use joy walking between classes. They report that it gives them a refreshing break from mental strain. They greet others along the walk and take in the beauty of nature and the surrounding architecture. Joy walking is a fun, easy, and practical way to practice mindfulness and positivity.

Nudge: take a joy walk

Simply 10 to 20 minutes of walking is enough to get you energized and refreshed. Try to keep the following in mind as you walk.

- Connect with your breath as you walk.

- Notice your stride and body posture.

- Walk with your arms relaxed with a gentle, natural swing.

- Assume a happy posture, one that is comfortable and relaxed with your gaze forward and slightly upward.

- As you walk, bring a smile to your mind. Take in the environment.

- Allow your eyes to smile gently.

- Bring a smile to your mouth as you connect with the natural beauty around you.

- Walk with awareness.

- Observe the environment, your posture, your breath, and your smile.

- Relax into the feeling of gratitude and joy as you continue to walk.

- Appreciate your surroundings as you awaken your senses with your awareness.

- Notice sounds, smells, landscape, sky, and the breeze as you walk.

- Feel free to acknowledge and smile at passersby.
- Allow the smile to cascade throughout your whole body.
- Feel your feet on the ground and notice the feeling you have at the moment.
- Feel the energy of your body as you walk.

Make Someone's Day

Appreciation makes everything better. Spend the time appreciating everything and everyone. Extend this essence of appreciation to all you meet during the course of the day. Use this energy of appreciation to create an intention to make someone's day in a small way. This does not have to be planned. Life will present many opportunities for you to make someone's day by doing some spontaneous gesture of kindness or generosity.

Our social environment can shift our direction downward toward gloom and doom. Just follow the news. Like a gusty wind, we can get swept away with negativity. I give my students an assignment to observe their conversations during the week and see who uplifts them and who is constantly complaining. I ask them to see if they can reduce their gossiping and complaining for one week. They return to class and share how simply bringing awareness to the quality of their conversations has allowed them to reduce stress and be more productive.

Notice how you might be inviting negative conversations into your space. See if you can shift your conversations to the positive. While we cannot direct the attitudes and actions of others, we can respond effectively by shifting toward the most uplifting response. See if you can change the direction of this destructive wind and redirect the sails to words that uplift and heal. Practice putting an end to gossiping and complaining and simply appreciate.

Don't worry when the curmudgeon voice interrupts. We all have a voice of judgment. Meet yours with a smile and move on. Take a deep breath and focus on grounding yourself; let go of tension and strain by using one of the breathing practices. Release and relax into the simplicity of the present moment. Look for the qualities in both your surroundings and your heart that invite feelings of gratitude and appreciation. Direct your mind to follow the train of thought that invokes self-kindness and compassion. The kinder we are to ourselves, the kinder we are to others.

There is a lot to love in our lives that we can share and receive. Use your intention to move into appreciation and soon you will naturally be making someone's day with very little effort. As you move through the day, look for things, people, and places to appreciate. Practicing appreciation invites the possibility of joy. What you bring to mind, you bring to life. We repeat what is familiar. Become familiar with the positive emotion of appreciation and let yourself be enthusiastic about it. Make your practice simply to make someone's day.

Appreciation has been researched by organizational psychologists and is used as a tool for positive organizational development in corporate cultures. These psychologists' research has demonstrated that feelings like hope, excitement, and joy increase creativity and cognitive flexibility in the workplace. Appreciation also promotes strong connections and cooperation between people.

Nudge: make someone's day this week

- For one week, live each day in full appreciation by paying attention to the positive.

- Shift your conversations to the positive.

- Write positive and uplifting e-mails and Facebook messages.

- Use the daily intention *I appreciate*.

- Generate thoughts and actions of appreciation.

- Say, "Thank you," or "Have a nice day."

- Allow gestures of spontaneous kindness.

Imagine a Good Day Mind Map

The mind loves images. Besides the hammock, two images I like to have in my life are the smiling fat-bellied Buddha and the hippie peace sign of the '60s. I grew up with the peace sign, and I love Buddhas—they make me think of the word *calm*. I have a peace sign on my refrigerator and a small Buddha in my office. These touchstones bring a smile to my face and create a soul-soothing feeling.

Consider: What images are you exposed to in your daily life? How can you add images into your life that support creating calm? Any image that brings you joy and reminds you of qualities of well-being will enhance your environment and inspire you. Begin to invite them into your life by making a collage, screen saver, or idea folder. Some people like to make an altar with images of spiritual figures. All of these practices and rituals have great value in grounding us to the qualities we can cultivate for greater calm and deeper connections. They are visual reminders to slow down.

Another powerful practice is visualization. Visualization is the simple activity of creating images in your mind and feelings in your body to represent your goals. Your mind can engage all five senses, creating all the images, sounds, scents, and feelings of a situation and environment in as much detail as you can. The focus is on the result.

Someone, years ago, gave me a magnet with the saying "Rest in your resolution." This pretty much sums it up. In your mind's eye, see your future as you relax. No wishing or wanting, just being with your future self for a few minutes a day can be powerful. Many athletes do this when they practice their sport; actors do it when they play a character. Entrepreneurs and business executives use visualization in scenario planning. While making a collage or vision board is popular and useful, I like the ease of daydreaming about some of the scenarios of my future life. I use all my senses to imagine the path to the end goal.

One of my friends once told me a story of when he was young and hitchhiking through Europe. When he stopped to admire a yacht, to his surprise he was invited in and given a tour and a brochure. He kept the brochure in a drawer by his bedside and would often look at it and admire the wood interior and the craftsmanship in the details of the yacht. He allowed himself to savor and enjoy the imagery surrounding this boat. Many years later, when he'd achieved fame and fortune, he ended up buying a yacht. To his surprise, after reviewing the paperwork and the name changes, it ended up being that same yacht he'd looked at many years ago.

While you might not make millions and buy a yacht, the lesson is to never underestimate the power of imagination. What might happen if you take five minutes a day to imagine well-being in your life?

Australian psychologist Alan Richardson demonstrated that a group who only visualized shooting baskets was just as good at the activity as the group who actually practiced shooting baskets. Positive psychologists have studied using your imagination for savoring an experience as a means to connect you to the future. Imagining a time in the future when you look back at your life with good memories can do this. The benefits of visualization include relaxation, increased productivity or skill, and increased happiness.

Nudge: make a "good day" mind map

Relax

- Relax and imagine the environment of your future best self.

- Think of specific areas of well-being and health.

- Using a first-person view, see and feel the details of your well-being.

- Imagine yourself looking back at your life with joy and contentment.
- Return. Allow yourself to come back, but stay with the feeling of your images.

Make

- Take a large sheet of paper and some colored markers.
- Write your main idea in the center of the paper and make a circle around it.
- Draw branches off the main idea and write down topics related to the main idea. Use the colored markers for different themes or ideas.
- Draw more branches from these and write your subtopics.
- Connect with all your senses: sight, taste, sound, and feelings. Draw images and symbols to represent ideas.
- Work on it until you have run out of ideas.

Reflect

- Take a break, or sleep on it, and review it the next day.
- Write about your ideas in your design notebook.

Make a Vision Board or Folder

One of the best ways to energize your visions is to put them in pictures. This is a way to mine your deep knowledge and wisdom from all corners of the mind. I have done this for many years in relation to my career. A vision board (sometimes called a treasure map or creativity collage) is a poster board filled with images and words that represent your goal. It is a fun, simple activity that puts you in the zone of relaxed attention. The idea behind it is to place images, words, and phrases of what you want on the board. This process of making a vision board is powerful because it creates positive feelings anchoring you to your goal with visual clarity.

If you lack time, you can do the same with a folder. When I created a vision folder about my desire to move to Charlottesville, Virginia, I merely filled a folder with pictures, articles, business cards, and news clippings related to Charlottesville. Occasionally I looked at my folder and spent time enjoying the images that inspired me. A former co-worker of mine had a similar dream. She wanted to move to Seattle, Washington. She heightened her desire by using a placemat that had a map of Seattle. Monday through Friday, she ate her lunch at her desk and dreamed about her move as she slowly savored her food. Soon she was vacationing in Seattle and eventually moved there.

Life changes begin with small actions. These are simple ways to remind and reenergize your feelings toward your goal. It is a part of the design process of making. There is no magic in creating a design board. It is about clarity, commitment, and creativity toward taking action steps to make your goals happen.

There are several ways to create a vision board. The following is one that I use in my classroom. My students enjoy making them, and this is the one class where they will happily stay late to complete their task. There is something wonderful about creating a collage and seeing your vision come alive with pictures and words. Time just flies by in this happy marriage of logic and imagination.

The process of collaging is relaxing and puts you in a state of active attention that psychologists call *flow*. Any activity in which you feel engaged, relaxed, and focused in the moment results in the state of flow. When I write or paint, I lose all track of time, as I am fully engaged and enjoying my work. You might reflect back and notice when this happens for you and how you can use this activity as a way to savor and appreciate your day.

If you don't have time to create a board, then create a vision folder; simply place anything that relates to your goal or dream in a folder rather than on a board. Then make sure you periodically take some time to savor and add new images and information.

Nudge: make a "happy at work" vision board or folder

Supplies: Half of a poster board, magazines, a glue stick, scissors, happy music (silence is fine, too)

Time: Two to three hours

- Relax, close your eyes, and choose a focus of "happy at work."

- Start with one minute of flipping through magazines and picking out images that represent your creative self. (Don't stop to think—just tear out what grabs your attention, even if it does not make sense.)

- Choose an image, then trim and paste it in the center of your poster board.

- Go through the magazines again, and tear out pictures that represent your "happy at work" intention. Even if it doesn't make sense, just have fun pulling out pictures that grab your attention. Keep them in a pile.

- Next, tear out words or phrases that grab your attention. Be quick and playful as you capture what is calling you.

- Review the images and words that you have gathered, then trim and paste the ones that you choose onto your board.

- Journal about your collage in your notebook.
- Savor your vision board. Keep it within view.

If you don't have time for a board or you want to try something new, try making a vision folder. The process is similar, but without the pasting onto a poster board—you just grab a folder and put inside your favorite clippings, articles, business cards, pictures, and brochures of the things you want to create in your life.

Act Great

Amy Cuddy is a Harvard business school professor and social psychologist who studies body language. In her popular 2012 TED talk, she explains that one important element of body language is the *power pose*. High-power poses are postures that open up the body. It's when we stand like Wonder Woman (with legs apart and hands on hips) or sit with our feet up on a desk. Low-power poses, in contrast, are postures in which we make ourselves smaller in an attempt to protect ourselves. Our poses not only affect how others perceive us, they actually change our body chemistry, and these changes affect the way we do our jobs and interact with people.

Since our body language affects how we perceive ourselves, why not shine? There are many ways to act great. Start with experimenting with the power poses that can be found in the video of Amy's TED talk online. Her research found that "our bodies change our minds, and our minds change our behavior, and our behavior changes our outcomes."

Striking a power pose can reduce symptoms of stress, improve performance, and increase confidence. Our imagination sparks with insights and inspires us to take action. It is important to take the leap of faith and dive into action toward our goals, even in the smallest ways.

Power posing can get you in the habit of taking action and making it joyful, curious, and productive. If you want a meaningful life, ally your imagination with action. Try out some of these poses that support bringing more joy, compassion, and brilliance into your life. In simple terms, begin with acting great.

We all have seen Ellen DeGeneres do this as she opens her television show. She does her little happy dance with the audience. Her power pose is dancing. It spreads some happiness, laughter, and love, creating positive energy. She wants her audience to have the value of a shifting of the energy upward. Happy dancing uplifts the spirit. Get your benevolent thought, sound, and movement going with a power pose or a dance.

Nudge: five ways to act great

- Stand like Wonder Woman with your hands on your hips and your legs separated.

- Do the victory pose with both arms above your head in a "V."

- Stand up when you are talking on the phone.

- Place your feet up on the desk with hands rested behind your head.

- Do a happy dance.

Grateful Heart

The quality of our lives is dictated by the state of our minds. Where we place our intention, our action follows. Positive psychologists have researched the many benefits that practices of gratitude have on our health and relationships. A focus on gratitude allows us to focus and cultivate qualities that form winning dispositions.

What are you grateful for?

To cultivate an authentic sense of appreciation, reflect on what you have received as well as what you have given to others. This focus on positivity directs our intention, attitudes, and actions.

There is an American Indian story about a boy talking to his grandfather. "Grandfather," he says, "What do you think about what's going on in the world?"

The grandfather gazes back at his grandson and replies, "I feel like the wolves are fighting in my heart. One is full of anger and one is full of love, forgiveness, and peace."

"So which one will win?" asks the boy.

The grandfather replies, "The one I feed."

Let's feed the practice of gratitude. Relaxation married to gratitude makes a great team. When we take time to relax and feel grateful for our breath and life, we affirm the beauty and meaning in our lives.

Gratitude is something that can be infused into your daily routine as well as your mental wanderings. If our mind's nature is to wander, why not have our mind wander around gratitude and possibilities? The mind likes direction, so give it a direction to follow.

Ask yourself, *Why is it so easy for me to be grateful?*

Let your mind wander into the specific details of why you are grateful. A grateful heart is an excellent way to relax the whole body with a feeling of deep satisfaction. The grateful-heart body scan allows for the flow of tension and calm—all equal information—to be noticed. As you let go, you shift from fighting yourself to allowing the mind and body to unwind. There are many ways to relax into gratitude. This is one of my favorites. This practice generates mindfulness and compassion with its focus on gratitude. The more you practice an evening gratitude, the more you direct your attention during the day to goodness. This practice can help as part of a healthy evening sleep routine.

Nudge: relax with a grateful heart

Read or record this practice, then use it nightly.

- Lie down in a comfortable place, watching your breathing.

- Take a stretch to lengthen your body and breath.

- Let your arms relax by your sides about four inches away from your body.

- Allow your legs and feet to drop and open up to the side.

- Let gravity hold you as you gently breathe.

- Start at the top of your head. Allow the muscles to soften and relax.

- Soften your forehead and your muscles around the eyes.

- Release your jaw by yawning.

- Move your awareness to your neck and shoulders.

- Continue softening and relaxing the shoulders, neck, and upper back.

- Follow down the back and allow your body to become heavy and relaxed.

- Relax into your belly and then let the legs soften and relax.

- Breathe and soften your muscles in the legs by paying attention.

- Finally, relax the muscles in your feet and toes.

- Recall a memory of gratitude. Take in all the elements and senses of the memory.

- Allow the feeling of gratitude to flood your body.

- Let go of the memory and rest in the feeling of gratefulness.

- Allow yourself 15 to 30 minutes to relax in this deep state of peace and gratitude.

Eat Real Food

Savoring our meals is an everyday mindfulness practice we all can do. Savoring is a positive activity for happiness. "Real foods" are simply whole foods that grow in the earth and that nourish your body, mind, and spirit. This food is locally and sustainably grown, organic, traditional, and seasonal. You can find this food sold at city markets and farmers' markets.

The real-food movement is trending now. It is a return to old-fashioned food, the food my grandparents served me in the '60s. I know many students who have formed groups, and they all take the trolley down to the city market on Saturdays and to grab lunch from a local farmer. They might savor some freshly made local burgers on the grill or head to the vendor who offers fresh lemonade and homemade tacos.

Whether you are growing your own garden or shopping at city or farmers' markets, this time spent tending or shopping involves savoring. Savor the relationships with the people around you and with the sights and smells of the earthiness of the food. Take little moments to savor while cooking. Take pleasure in the air you are breathing, a look on someone's face, or the flavors and textures of your meal. When we get into the habit of savoring, we are naturally drawn to fresh, wholesome foods.

I love going to the Charlottesville City Market on Saturday morning and talking with the farmers about their seasonal offerings and how to cook them. Part of the experience of learning about the food is getting to know the farmers and their stories. In turn, they get to know me, and I often find extra treats in my canvas bag. The market is a rich community-based experience that supports the local economy, builds connections, and enhances well-being.

If you have not already gone, I urge you to take a trip to a city or farmers' market and spend some time getting to know the vendors. I promise you will be surprised by who is producing the food in your community. They are former scientists, Wall Street executives, lawyers, recent college graduates, and engineers. They have diverse backgrounds and they relish sharing information and a taste of the good life.

The local city or farmers' markets are one of the ways to change your lifestyle by incorporating real food—freshly grown rather than processed foods. These are whole foods with little or no processing. Think local fruits and vegetables, meats, eggs, and cheeses, to name a few. The buzzwords for this real food movement include *community-based, local, green, fair-trade, artisanal,* and *slow food.* Real food is savoring. This food is so fresh and tasty that it needs minimal additions when cooked.

Nudge: take your time savoring a meal with a variety of whole foods

Plan some time to sit and savor a real food meal with friends or family.

- When eating, sit and begin by smelling and looking at your plate.

- Share your observations with your friends or family. Listen to their comments.

- Notice all aspects of the food: flavor, colors, aroma, and the feeling it gives you.

- Notice the nourishment and satisfaction in a few bites.

- Allow some pauses to savor your food by taking in the taste, smells, texture, and beauty.

- Eat slowly and enjoy conversation. Stop when satisfied, not full.

- Savor and space your bites with curiosity.

Next pick a meal or snack to eat alone, slowly, mindfully, in silence.

Drink Water

Water is a wellness tool for energy, weight loss, deeper sleep, and pain reduction. Most of us are dehydrated and in need of some fresh plain water. After all, the body is mainly water; it needs water to work effectively. Water washes toxins from your body to increase energy.

When I go a day without monitoring my water intake, my energy zaps and I am exhausted. Many of us are walking around dragging due to the lack of water. When I drink water throughout the day, I find my physical and mental energy increases.

Dehydration contributes to the cause of headaches and back pain. Your brain needs water to think clearly, be alert, and concentrate. We are more productive when we are well hydrated. Get a water filter and a fun container and make drinking water a priority. Water helps fuel the muscles when exercising by keeping your joints and muscles well lubricated.

Make drinking water a habit by taking some sips of water throughout the day. Like anything, you don't want to overdo it with water. Keep it simple and start slow. Have a glass by your bed and drink from it when you wake in the morning or sip on it if you wake in the middle of the night. Have a glass before you leave home in the morning and then one later in the afternoon. Drink an hour before dinner or on your drive home. See how you can add water to your daily routine. One simple way to increase your water intake is to eat more fresh fruits and vegetables, as they do contain water.

Eight to ten cups of water per day is the average amount needed, depending on your size and activity level. If you exercise, take saunas, or are just active and sweating, you will need a couple extra cups. A good place to start is with six cups a day—use common sense to know when to add more water. If you are out working in the hot sun, in the garden or some other location, have a water bottle close by and take breaks to drink and stretch.

A beauty tip for great skin is to develop a habit of drinking water. Water replenishes skin tissues, moisturizes, and increases elasticity. Water is needed for the effectiveness of all the body systems, especially digestion and the immune system. When our bodies are hydrated and systems are working effectively, then they feel good and create that happy, good-mood feeling. Staying hydrated is one of the simplest, easiest, and cheapest things we can do to maintain our energy and vitality.

Nudge: make mindful water drinking a practice

- Take water with you to work and when you're out running errands.
- Sip water slowly throughout the day.
- Use a cup or bottle that you like.
- Substitute water for other beverages. I like hot water with lemon and honey.
- Keep water handy around your house and at work.
- Experiment with flavors by adding fruit or herbs like mint, lemon, lime, or berries.

Happy Driving

Happy driving is about taking responsibility for ourselves and using our skill of noticing feelings, responses, and actions we make while driving. By all means drive, but drive defensively. Look around, pay attention, and avoid the poor drivers. Use the time you have alone in the car to enjoy music, listen to a radio show or an audiobook, or just daydream, making the next part of your day the best.

What about road rage? Have you developed a habit of getting angry with other drivers in cars? Many of my students have shared that this is a problem for them. As I said before, anything we practice we get better at it. When we practice anger, we get better at it. You may need to take a new vantage point on driving and see how you can turn it into a calming, enjoyable, and productive experience. If you are an irritated driver, the first step will be to apply some mindful awareness and compassion as you notice which of your emotions are triggers on the road, and how they trigger you.

What are the things you are saying to yourself?

Driving with awareness reduces road rage, accidents, and running out of gas. When we pay attention, we know when to fill up the tank; we slow down, and we breathe away anger or frustration.

We cannot control how other people drive. So many are mindlessly talking on their cell phones, not giving their full attention to the road. Maybe you are one of them. Think about how you can enjoy driving without your phone or other devices interrupting your attention. Do you want to control your cell phone—or are you going to let it control you?

When you practice self-control, you get better at it. Neurons that fire together, over time wire together. For many of us, our cell phones have created a deep-seated itch to keep checking them. We are built to create habits. You just have to be aware of the habit you are creating. Constantly checking your cell phone can be distracting, and while driving it can be very dangerous.

One of my favorite things to do is to break a bad habit. In this case, I might make it my personal rule to shut my phone off while driving, thus allowing for no disruptions. When I get to my destination, I can check the messages. If that seems too extreme, then at least don't look at the phone while driving. If it goes off, pull off the road before checking it. Honestly, this behavior can save lives.

The benefits of happy driving are fewer accidents, more pleasure, and enhanced productivity.

Nudge: drive happy

- Start with an intention of happy driving.

- Create the conditions for a calm drive by slowing down to avoid bad drivers and other hazards. Be mindfully aware of your surroundings.

- Turn off your cell phone and resist checking it at stoplights.

- Make the drive enjoyable. Play happy music.

- Hydrate. Bring a water bottle when you hit the road.

- Take the time to imagine the best possible outcome for your relationships and projects.

Go Outside and Play

Nature is restorative. Our environment influences our energy and imagination. We are meant to go outside, get fresh air, and connect with nature. We tend to feel better outside, which makes us feel better on the inside. While physical movement is necessary, so is just going outside to play in nature. Take a break from striving for a perfect exercise routine, and allow yourself to focus on the joy of being active. Explore and appreciate the natural world.

This could be as simple as spending time in your garden, taking a walk down the street, or going for a hike in the woods.

When you get outside and move, you expose yourself to nature, beauty, and connection to other people. Your energy is brighter and expands.

I ask my students to unplug from their electronics as they walk to class and simply be present with their surroundings. After a week of this practice, they come back and share with me that they'd forgotten how beautiful the campus is and they are so thrilled to reconnect with its beauty. Before, they were oblivious to friends on the path to class and now they stop to smile and chat. Walking becomes a simple and easy way to reduce stress and provide a sense of renewal in their busy day.

I remind my students to gaze upward on their walks as well to appreciate the architecture, sky, and landscape. This posture of bringing the gaze upward is also of value as it lifts the mood. When you can make your walk playful and observant, it transforms you. It becomes a practice these students use well beyond their college years.

What outdoor activities and outings create joy on a daily basis? Notice how you feel as you focus on a world of beauty.

Nudge: give yourself a green hour

- Spend at least an hour a day outside.
- Work in the garden.
- Walk in the neighborhood.
- Take a walk, a hike, a bike ride. Go canoeing or kayaking.
- Join an outdoor fitness group or community garden.

A Good Night's Sleep

Sleep is my beauty secret. Sleep is vital to feeling great. A good night's sleep can reduce stress and regulate your hormone levels to balance mood and emotions. Being tired makes it harder to be happy and wreaks havoc on the hormones, creating a cycle of stress. Brain experts are always touting the benefits of a good night's sleep for memory health. I recently heard Dr. Rubin Naiman speak about how our lifestyle has significantly disrupted our sleep routines. He said, "We probably need about 8 hours and 15 minutes on average. I'm always fond of the hidden fact that Albert Einstein slept 10 hours a night, and it didn't seem to hurt his productivity."

Sleep is a key time for your brain's neurons to make lasting interconnections. Sleep is a great source of nourishment for the body. It is a time time when tissue repair and growth are heightened as our bodies repair and restore themselves after all of the stressors of the day. Sleep, like good nutrition and exercise, is an essential component of a healthy lifestyle.

One of the best ways to jump-start your commitment to sleep and balance your hormones is to take a sleep retreat, a long weekend where you do nothing but sleep. Four days of getting to bed by 9 P.M. and sleeping until you wake up naturally will do wonders for your energy and resetting your sleep cycle. Implement change gradually. As with anything new, undertake small, happy, daily steps to support change. Try getting to bed five minutes earlier each night. Slowly but surely, you will create a healthy and satisfying sleep routine that is energizing and refreshing.

Getting a good night's sleep is one of the easiest ways to feel great. The rule of thumb is to get seven to nine hours of sleep. And yes, naps do count! If you take a short catnap in the middle of the day, around 3 P.M. for 10 to 20 minutes, you will be refreshed. An afternoon nap can energize you and help you focus in the afternoon.

Develop a sleep routine that works for you. Strive to go to bed by 10 P.M. When we stay up late, our bodies make extra cortisol, which contributes to insulin resistance and creates belly fat. Instead of hopping into bed after a long day, take time to unwind early in the evening.

Do something relaxing in low light for 30 to 60 minutes before bed. Avoid doing anything stimulating, such as surfing the Internet, reading a suspense novel, or having an intense conversation. Doing things like taking a relaxing bath, having a cup of herbal tea, reading, or making time for intimacy can soothe you into a slumber. If you have trouble with ruminating, take some time to write down your worries and any creative solutions. Let yourself know that you don't need to think about them now; you can always come back to them in the morning. Practice self-care and make sleep a priority.

Nudge: simple habits to help you get a good night's sleep

- To sleep well, it helps to get some exercise during the day. Movement helps all functions of the body. We are meant to move, not sit all day.

- Create a relaxation routine or sleep ritual to slow down your evening. Try a short relaxation body scan, an Epsom salt bath, or journaling your worries.

- Create a restful place to sleep. Sleep in a quiet, cool, dark, and comfortable room that is free of noise and disruption. Sleep on a comfortable mattress and get blackout curtains.

- Create an environment for a sound sleep. Make your bedroom a sanctuary.

- Avoid excess light from things like computers a few hours before bed. Keep the lighting low in the evening. Softening the lights before bedtime can encourage the flow of melatonin. (I occasionally add a supplement of melatonin to my sleep routine.)

- Avoid alcohol and caffeine in the afternoon and night. Caffeine is a stimulant that affects the sympathetic nervous system and can stay in your body for up to 12 hours. Drinking caffeine after lunch will increase your cortisol and make it hard for you to wind down for bed.

- Try to find some fun, satisfying beverages like mineral water or the new probiotic drinks that have a zip without the zing. Drink plenty of pure water. Try an herbal tea. Sedative herbs like valerian and chamomile can significantly decrease the time it takes to fall asleep.

- Practice slow deep breathing as you relax under the warmth of the covers.

afterword

I recently was a guest speaker in a class at the Morven Summer Institute. After my talk on mindfulness, several students came up to me to share how they like to slow down and relax.

One student said, "Do you know what my friends and I like to do to relax? We like hammocking. Resting in a hammock. In fact, I like hammocking so much I contacted the ENO Company to see if I could be a campus rep."

I smiled and told him, "Wow. *Hammocking* is a verb! That is so cool."

Over the years, I have savored my relaxing time in a hammock, and I'm glad to see it's trending on university campuses. I have noticed an influx of ENO hammocks around the University of Virginia grounds. While outside on the university grounds I am seeing hammocks, inside the walls of classrooms I have noticed an increase in programs that teach and use design thinking principles and mindfulness practices.

There is a mindfulness movement in our country creating a wave of communities that value the quality of a calm, balanced mind in our schools, government, and businesses. And on a parallel path, designers have created a maker movement, which values the design elements in a social environment with an emphasis on learning through doing. Community interaction, shared knowledge, and encouraging exploration of novel with traditional ideas build the maker's mind-set for creativity. This mistake-positive and team approach calls for a level of thoughtfulness, communication, and community building that can be gleaned from the *mindfulness movement.* Both movements adhere to the beginner's mind of seeing each moment with fresh eyes. And both the maker movement and the mindfulness movement require practice, reflection, and community.

Modern relaxation, mindfulness, and positivity are about making the practice work for you and your schedule. It can be difficult to carve out a large amount of time for hammocking, meditation, journaling, or healthy eating. Waiting for the conditions to be ideal will lead you to procrastinate. By creating or joining a community, you get support, new knowledge, and accountability. Also, by taking small, happy, and daily steps, you build the momentum and cultivate a greater capacity for joy, compassion, and brilliance.

The solution is to start by doing several one-minute practices a day or work on one keystone habit, like creating that great new sleep routine. Keystone habits are powerful because they have a domino effect on your day. More sleep means more energy, and that can change many things in your life.

Designers believe in taking creative sabbaticals or at least unplugging from technology for a few hours. When the world is coming at us with rapid-pace e-mails, non-stop phone calls, and other interruptions, we move into a reactive state. The more you periodically disconnect and relax, the more you create a space for insight and connection.

As an educator, I know students need time in the learning process to let new ideas incubate. By providing brain breaks in the classroom, we see recall is much higher. There is value in the familiar adage: "I think I will sleep on it." Psychologists have written about the value of taking a brain break every hour as a way for letting information assimilate and integrate with older memories. In the business world, the old model of powering through a problem or meeting is becoming obsolete if a company adheres to the science and value of creativity.

The *Discover, Make, Do* sections in this book support personal responsibility in transforming our lives. They give a method and a practice to slow down in order to create or innovate. Downtimes are doing something very valuable and necessary, allowing our bodies to function in an optimal way. Here is my simple approach to creative problem solving using the mindful designer's mind-set:

- *Take it all in:* Practice mindfulness to observe and see beyond the ordinary.

- *Take note:* Write, draw, and scribble thoughts and ideas.

- *Take a break:* Let go in order for insight to arrive.

- *Take a risk:* Trust your instincts and take action.

I don't need to have all the perfect answers, but I do need to experiment, be bold, and have patience as I allow ideas, thoughts, and solutions to emerge. The unfolding of life requires intention, attention, and calmness. The design-thinking elements (*discover, make, do*) provide a new way of creating opportunities for transformational change that are self-compassionate and sustainable because they are mistake-positive. There is no wrong way; *doing* is what is important.

Life transforms through practice. See how the practices work for you and stick with them. My university students encouraged me to write this book. Their enthusiasm is what fueled my dedication as an educator, speaker, and writer. I hope you find joy, compassion, and brilliance in your life and share it with others.

Enjoy the journey!

recommended reading

Here are a few of the books that I have used in my Mindful Leadership course and in other programs I teach. Every year, new research has informed my teaching. Each course may be similar in design, but the content is informed by research and student projects. This is a list of my students' favorite books to learn more about design thinking and the three elements of designing calm: joy, compassion, and brilliance.

Relaxation

Minding the Body, Mending the Mind by Dr. Joan Borysenko

The Relaxation Response by Dr. Herbert Benson and Miriam Z. Klipper

How God Changes Your Brain by Dr. Andrew Newberg and Mark Waldman

Mindfulness

10 Mindful Minutes by Goldie Hawn and Wendy Holden

Cultivating Compassion by Jeffrey Hopkins

The Miracle of Mindfulness by Thich Nhat Hanh

Full Catastrophe Living: Using the Wisdom of Your Body and Mind to Face Stress, Pain, and Illness by Jon Kabat-Zinn and Thich Nhat Hanh

Positivity

Positivity by Barbara L. Fredrickson

Finding Flow by Mihaly Csikszentmihalyi

The Willpower Instinct by Kelly McGonigal

CrazyBusy by Edward M. Hallowell

The Happiness Hypothesis: Finding Modern Truth in Ancient Wisdom by Jonathan Haidt

Flourish by Martin E. P. Seligman

Design Thinking

Glimmer by Warren Berger

The Laws of Simplicity by John Maeda

A Whole New Mind by Daniel H. Pink

Change by Design by Tim Brown

Leadership

More Balls Than Hands: Juggling Your Way to Success by Learning to Love Your Mistakes by Michael J. Gelb

Primal Leadership by Daniel Goleman, Richard Boyatzis, and Annie McKee

The Fifth Discipline: The Art & Practice of the Learning Organization by Peter M. Senge

Presence: An Exploration of Profound Change in People, Organizations, and Society by Peter M. Senge, C. Otto Scharmer, Joseph Jaworski, and Betty Sue Flowers

acknowledgments

I was wondering if I should attend the Hay House event "How to Write a Book Proposal" in Asheville, North Carolina. Then I had a dream that woke me up and told me the answer. It only shouted the name "Reid Tracy." I went to the conference and did not realize it came with a contest to win a book contract. So, like many others, several months later I submitted my book proposal. The morning of the announcement, the phone rang. The first words I heard were, "Marga, this is Reid Tracy. I would like to welcome you to the Hay House family."

A very special thanks to Reid Tracy and the amazing Hay House family for supporting this book project, allowing me to reach many more people than I thought possible. Many thanks to Shannon Littrell, Stacey Smith, Christy Salinas, Charles McStravick, Nicolette Salamanca Young, Angela Moody, and Lisa Bernier.

I am grateful for so many students and teachers, as well as my parents, family, and friends who have supported my journey. Thank you to my colleagues Brad Brown, Jill Jones, and Jeffrey Walker, who supported my work in teaching mindfulness and in writing this book.

Many thanks to my writing coaches, Kristen-Paige Madonia, who helped me birth this book at the same time she was having her first baby, and Nell Boeschenstein, who pushed me to think deeper and write happier. And, a big thank-you to special friends and fellow writers, Jenny Zenner, Julie Gronlund, Emily Robey Morrison, and Denise Stewart, who cheered me on, advised, edited, and, most important, believed in me 100 percent.

A big shout-out of love and gratitude to friends Sarah Cramer Shields whose keen eyes can capture magic with photography and Mary Michaela Murray who added her design aesthetic to the book cover.

A heartfelt thank-you to my dear friends Pam and Lee Marraccini who fed me and made me laugh at least once a week, and to Rob McGinnis, who surrounded me with love.

Lastly, special thanks to Goldie Hawn for her friendship, encouragement, and support.

about the author

Marga Odahowski is a nationally known wellness and mindfulness trainer, speaker, and coach. She has served on the faculty of the University of Virginia for over 20 years, working with students to reduce stress and build habits to increase calmness, creativity, and connection. She has developed programs and courses that support all aspects of health, including the most powerful and least taught: the power of mindfulness. Marga has taught mindfulness in several departments throughout the University of Virginia, including mindfulness programs for the MBA for Executives program in the Darden School of Business.

Please visit her website at www.marga.com.

We hope you enjoyed this Hay House book. If you'd like to receive our online catalog featuring additional information on Hay House books and products, or if you'd like to find out more about the Hay Foundation, please contact:

Published and distributed in Australia by: Hay House Australia
Pty. Ltd., 18/36 Ralph St., Alexandria NSW 2015 • *Phone:* 612-
9669-4299 • *Fax:* 612-9669-4144 • www.hayhouse.com.au

Published and distributed in the United Kingdom by:
Hay House UK, Ltd., Astley House, 33 Notting Hill Gate, London
W11 3JQ • *Phone:* 44-20-3675-2450 • *Fax:* 44-20-3675-2451
www.hayhouse.co.uk

Published and distributed in the Republic of South Africa by:
Hay House SA (Pty), Ltd., P.O. Box 990, Witkoppen 2068
Phone/Fax: 27-11-467-8904 • info@hayhouse.co.za

Published in India by: Hay House Publishers India, Muskaan
Complex, Plot No. 3, B-2, Vasant Kunj, New Delhi 110 070
Phone: 91-11-4176-1620 • *Fax:* 91-11-4176-1630
www.hayhouse.co.in

Distributed in Canada by: Raincoast Books, 2440 Viking Way,
Richmond, B.C. V6V 1N2 • *Phone:* 1-800-663-5714
Fax: 1-800-565-3770 • www.raincoast.com

$\sim\!\!\!\prec$

Take Your Soul on a Vacation

Visit www.HealYourLife.com® to regroup, recharge,
and reconnect with your own magnificence.
Featuring blogs, mind-body-spirit news, and life-changing
wisdom from Louise Hay and friends.

Visit www.HealYourLife.com today!